AWAKENING

• • •

Jin Lan Cera

©2023 JIN LAN CERA

ALL RIGHTS RESERVED

ISBN: 978-0-9989899-6-9

AUTHORED BY JIN LAN CERA

EDITED BY ANNA WATSON

COVER DESIGNED BY: ALEXANDER VALCHEV

This book is dedicated to my beloved father, Deng Ji Xiang, and to those who struggle in the darkness of life and search for light.

Contents

I. Preface………………………………….……….....……..1

II. The Journey To Awakening…….…..………...…...…..9
    - Discover The Law of Attraction
    - Stricking Life Science Experiments
    - The Buddha's Teachings

III. The 3 Steps To Manifest Our Dream…………..159
    - Raise our frequency
        - Quiet our mind
        - Be positive
        - Envision a mission-oriented life
    - Broadcast
        - Stay positive
        - Say the keywords of our dream
        - Give what we want
    - Receive
        - Be grateful
        - Be mindful
        - Allow good things to happen

IV. Afterword………………………………………171

PREFACE

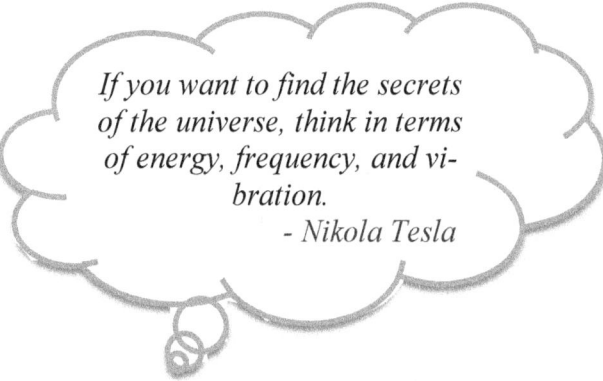

If you want to find the secrets of the universe, think in terms of energy, frequency, and vibration.
  - Nikola Tesla

Dear Reader,

Why am I writing this book? Because I've stumbled upon some exhilarating revelations that I'm eager to share with you. These insights have the potential to guide you in bringing your dream life into the realm of reality, just as my own life underwent a remarkable transformation after everything seemingly fell apart in 2020.

As the waves of the COVID-19 pandemic washed over the U.S., I found myself caught in a maelstrom of adversity: my health deteriorated, my career crumbled, and a 16-year marriage came to an end. Undoubtedly, it was the darkest period I had ever endured, and the agony was particularly acute for someone with a deep-seated sense of pride.

In my quest for guidance, I turned my gaze to the Universe. A figure self-identified as Abraham Hikes[1] emerged on YouTube, delivering a series of thought-provoking lectures. However, the depth of her discourse often required multiple revisits to grasp truly. Amid her talks, the term "**The Law of Attraction**" surfaced frequently, radiating an aura of immense potency. Yet, to my bewilderment, I had never encountered this concept before.

Eager to unravel this enigma, I delved into online research and immersed myself in Rhonda Byrne's book, "*The Secret*."[2] It eloquently expounded upon **The Law of Attraction**, positioning it as a fundamental law of Nature. But what, precisely, does

---

[1] https://www.youtube.com/@AbrahamHicks

[2] https://en.wikipedia.org/wiki/The_Secret_(Byrne_book)

this law entail? Allow me to present my distilled understanding:

The Law of Attraction unfolds as a discernible pattern embedded within the fabric of Nature, intrinsically linked with the tenets of New Thought[3] philosophy.

This pattern unveils three pivotal truths:

1. Thoughts are vibrational energy.
2. Similar thoughts attract each other due to synchronicity of similar frequency.
3. People could enhance/impair health, wealth, and relationships with this law.

---

[3] New Thought was seen by its adherents as succeeding "ancient thought", accumulated wisdom and philosophy from a variety of origins, such as Ancient Greek, Roman, Egyptian, Chinese, Taoist, Vedic, Hindu, and Buddhist cultures and their related belief systems, primarily regarding the interaction among thought, belief, consciousness in the human mind, and the effects of these within and beyond the human mind.

https://en.wikipedia.org/wiki/New_Thought

This concept felt familiar, like a memory echoing from my past. It reminded me of a chemistry experiment I once experienced at Western Nevada College. It was the Double Slit Experiment[4], and its discoveries echoed the way how things are connected. Just like how people's actions and thoughts can affect each other, quantum particles in the experiment showed how they can change the outcomes.

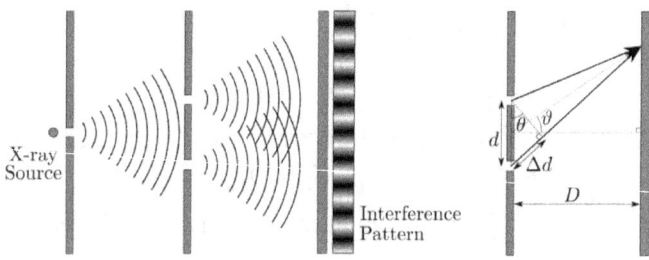

Double Slit Experiment Explained in Graph

This experiment taught us that every tiny particle vibrates. It also showed that when two waves with identical frequency move together in the same direction, their combined outcome becomes stronger at building up or breaking things apart. This is why the people in our proximity can evoke either our

---

[4] https://en.wikipedia.org/wiki/Double-slit_experiment

finest qualities or our weaknesses. It's also the reason wise leaders unite individuals for constructive endeavors, whereas unwise leaders gather them to fight what's unjust. This dynamic is reflected in the prosperity of certain societies, in contrast to the turmoil endured by others trapped in ceaseless discord.

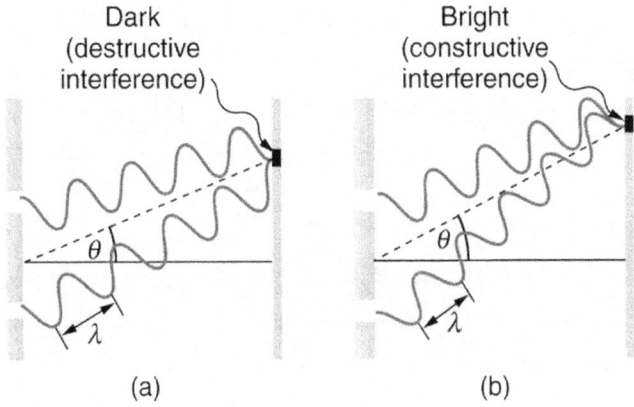

Double Slit Experiment

Nonetheless, I find myself unable to fully concur with every assertion made in Rhonda Byrne's book. An instance lies in her claim that envisioning one's desires and believing they will manifest suffices, with no requirement to comprehend the process of realization. Supposedly, the universe would ensure the fruition of our dreams. However, upon delving into my research, I've uncovered discrepancies in this proposition.

This idea is proven wrong by the experiences of Ms. Sun Chu Lin[5], who has amazing mental abilities and is a lifelong researcher in life science at the China University of Geoscience. She can use her mind power to make deep-fried peanuts come back to life and grow more than an inch in a few minutes. However, even though she's so powerful, she still must follow the regular steps of how things naturally grow. She can make things grow faster, but she can't skip the normal stages of growth.

During a television interview, Professor Lee Si Chen[6], the former president of National Taiwan University, who had collaborated with Ms. Sun Chu Lin on life science research for many years, shared an interesting insight. He mentioned that they attempted a similar experiment on wheat seeds, like the one they did with the fried peanuts. Despite their efforts, the experiment didn't yield the desired results.

---

[5] https://www.ictmhw.com/en/copy-of-7

[6] https://en.wikipedia.org/wiki/Lee_Si-chen

After seeking guidance from a biologist, they learned that wheat follows a different growth pattern compared to peanuts. The biologist explained that wheat needs to develop its root system before the sprouts can start growing. With this new understanding, the research team modified their experimental approach accordingly. As a result of these adjustments, Ms. Sun Chu Lin successfully grew wheat sprouts from seeds within one hour.

Even though many people doubted the ideas in *"The Secret"* and Wikipedia claimed the **Law of Attraction** pseudoscience, my own exploration gave me a chain of positive surprises. It turns out that the **Law of Attraction,** the idea that our thoughts can shape our lives, is based on scientific principles. The evidence I discovered was way beyond my craziest imagination. What started as me trying to understand **The Law of Attraction** and use it to solve my practical problems, the path led me to an amazing journey of spiritual awakening while receiving the life of my dreams.

Thus, dear reader, I am delighted to present to you the delectable and nourishing fruits that have sprung forth from my spiritual odyssey. As you journey through this book, you will discover my modified rendition of Rhonda Byrne's three steps to manifest your dream: *Ask, Believe,* and *Receive*, which I've transformed into *Raise Our Frequency, Broadcast, and Receive*. I delve into the reasons behind these adjusted steps and how they can better guide you, offering a detailed exploration. May you relish the reading experience, and may you come to realize that a splendid new life awaits you.

THE JOURNEY TO AWAKENING

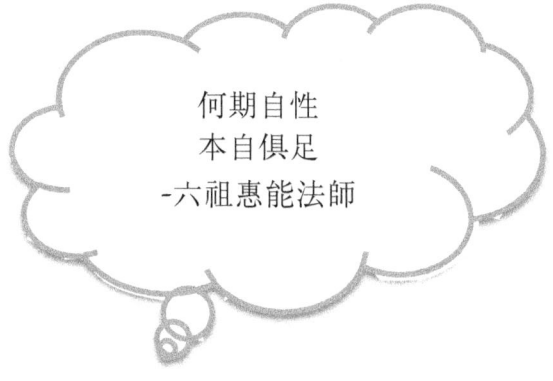

何期自性
本自俱足
-六祖惠能法師

"Who would have thought that our Buddha nature is intrinsically self-sufficient!"
~ *Hui-Neng Grand Master of Zen*

I was born and raised in China during the 1960s, in a society where atheism was the norm. I have a deep affection for science and a strong belief in its principles. During my college years in the United States, I excelled in science courses like physics, chemistry, and biology, earning straight A grades. I surf on YouTube documentaries about cosmology and quantum physics almost daily. To convince me of something, tangible evidence needs to be presented right in front of me; otherwise, it's hard for me to believe.

So, when I came across a line in Rhonda Byrne's book that claimed I could effortlessly receive my biggest material dream without understanding how, I felt a strong skepticism. How could that possibly be true? This doubt led me to delve deeper and continue seeking answers. This journey began when everything in my life seemed to be falling apart.

Discovering The Law of Attraction:

Pain

Life hit me like a never-ending storm of challenges, one after another, each more intense than the last. It felt as if the universe had conspired to push me to my limits, testing my physical and mental strength. Over the past decade, I found myself caught in a whirlwind of emotions and struggles, a journey that would define my existence.

I felt utterly helpless, watching my ex-husband struggle with a string of unsuccessful procedures, including a failed knee replacement and two more surgeries to fix it, as I stood by his side. I was left feeling helpless and desperate to comfort him after witnessing the agony of his battle with bipolar depression and its persistent hold, which ultimately led to his hospitalization owing to the spectra of suicidal thoughts.

A new kind of conflict was going on inside the boundaries of my own body. My spine had two slipped discs, which made even the smallest movements excruciatingly painful. Unrelenting pain served as a constant reminder of my mortality and vulnerability. Even while I was physically hurting, I found myself trying to deal with the emotional toll it had taken. Each stride was a monument to the perseverance needed to endure.

Amid these personal difficulties, I started a perilous voyage through the world of employment. I sent thousands of job applications, each one a glimpse of hope, with optimism as my guide. However, the comments I got - or the lack thereof - made me question my value for this society. Numerous interviews that initially seemed promising later turned into disappointment, leading me to wonder what good I could possibly do in a world that seemed determined to keep its doors shut.

The threat of losing our home loomed over us like a storm cloud, casting a shadow of uncertainty over our lives. The banks' consideration of foreclosure felt like an impending doom, and the weight of this impending loss pressed down upon me, threatening to crush any semblance of stability I clung to.

As if the weight of these struggles wasn't enough, the intricate web of my ex-husband's previous marriages added another layer of complexity to my emotional landscape. Their ungrateful attitude toward my contribution to this family made me question the meaning of life. We came to the difficult decision of going forward with an amicable divorce during this upheaval. The decision resulted from a shared wish to escape the excruciating suffering that had become our shared existence.

I found myself traversing a maze of feelings in those moments of despair, including pain, irritation, helplessness, and the sour taste of injustice. It was a period of profound darkness that seemed to stretch on indefinitely, testing the limits of my resilience. And yet, it was within this darkness that the spark of curiosity and the yearning for a deeper understanding of the Universe and life began to flicker, illuminating the path that would eventually lead me to discover the transformative power of the **Law of Attraction.**

As if the challenges I faced weren't already overwhelming, the arrival of the COVID-19 pandemic added yet another layer of complexity to my tumultuous journey. It was as if the world had plunged into chaos, and I found myself standing at the precipice of homelessness, teetering on the edge of an abyss I never thought I'd encounter.

In June 2020, I finally got a job as an advocate at a homeless shelter in Reno, NV. Stepping into this environment, I was immediately confronted with the harsh realities that many individuals faced daily. The stories I heard, and the lives I witnessed were a stark reminder of the fragility of our circumstances and the thin line that separated each of us from the brink of despair.

Despite the toxicity that often pervaded the shelter's environment, I determined to dedicate myself wholeheartedly to the cause. It was a commitment that went beyond mere duty; it was fueled by a deep-seated desire to make a difference to the society and myself. This dedication led me to pour myself into my work, surpassing even the levels of effort I had invested during my past experiences as a successful businesswoman in China and as a diligent economics student at Wellesley College.

I noticed that I was consistently testing the limits of my own strength. I worked harder than anyone else. When the colleagues were playing video games, I was cleaning up every corner of the facility, although that was not in my job description because I had passionately embraced this cause. I did so because I genuinely cared about the people I met and believed that any action, no matter how tiny, could have a significant impact on their lives.

The challenges I faced during this period were not only external but also internal. The emotional toll of witnessing the struggles of those around me weighed heavily on my heart. It was as if their suffering became my own, and even after my workday was over, I continued to feel the effects of their experiences. And yet, during this emotional turbulence, I discovered an unwavering resilience within myself—an unyielding spirit that refused to be defeated by the overwhelming odds stacked against us.

Little did I know that this immersion in the world of those who were battling for their very survival would serve as a profound catalyst for my own journey of self-discovery and transformation. The lessons I learned, and the insights I gained while navigating the lives of others would become integral to understanding the principles of the **Law of Attraction**, setting the stage for a journey that would forever alter the course of my life.

Light

Imagine being trapped in a cycle of misery, desperately seeking an escape. That was my life until the Universe whispered a secret through Esther Hicks[7]: the **Law of Attraction.** Yet, because I had always held onto the belief in materialism, my grasp of the **Law of Attraction** remained centered on the physical aspects of life. It wasn't until a series of striking events unfolded at the end of 2022 that my perspective shifted dramatically. These events were so impactful that they transformed me in ways I

---

[7] https://en.wikipedia.org/wiki/Esther_Hicks

could never have anticipated. Now, the world and my understanding of myself have forever changed.

Embarking on a scientific journey, I delved deep into the **Law of Attraction**. This cosmic insight took me on an exciting ride. Esther Hicks, my first new star, added cosmic brilliance to my journey. July 2021 brought Ken, my true love, into my life — a twist I might have missed without the guidance of her light.

The **Law of Attraction** took the lead role in life's grand theatre, turning my love life into an enchanting cosmic tale. Science, mysticism, and destiny danced together, scripting a love story that surpassed even my wildest dreams. A heartfelt nod to the **Law of Attraction,** the ultimate matchmaker, and to those who paved the cosmic path to my "happily ever after"! Now, let's explore how I bridged science and mysticism in the next chapter of this remarkable journey.

Pain

Feelings are like colors painting the canvas of our lives. They're what make us human, connecting us to the moments we cherish and those we wish to forget and forgive. Now, I am diving into the world of these feelings, where our hearts and souls reveal their nature. It's a journey through the emotions that define us, where we explore the depths of what it means to be human.

In the early days of October 2022, Ken and I were revelling in the vibrant energy of New York City. However, when I received a call from my second brother, Rong, in Chongqing, China, with grave news, our world abruptly changed. Rong told me that our mother had suffered a crippling fall and was now confined to a bed. Even worse, as our father was attempting to get Mom some medicine, he had an accident. He slipped and hurt his head, compounding the hardship we were already experiencing.

Fortunately, a sympathetic bystander who saw my father's predicament quickly dialed an ambulance. Father was sent immediately to Chongqing Emergency Hospital. I felt a deep sadness and a strong desire to be with my parents, but an obstacle stood in my way. My visa had been halted due to Covid-19, and I requested a special visa to visit them urgently.

The waiting was excruciating as the weight of my guilt bore down on me relentlessly. Father had given us everything he had, pouring his heart and soul into our well-being, yet when he needed me the most, I was absent. Personal struggles and the unrelenting grip of the pandemic had led me astray, causing me to forsake him for a painful stretch of five years. The burden of my inactions was unforgivable in my own eyes, making it impossible to find solace. Sleep became a distant luxury, with each night haunted by a barrage of nightmares that served as a cruel reminder of my failures.

Every day and night, I fervently prayed for Father's well-being, seeking solace in the idea that perhaps some higher power would intervene. I reached out to friends and family, imploring them to join me in these prayers, even though I had no understanding of how such divine mechanisms operated. I clung to the desperate hope that some sort of magic could work its way into my beloved father's life.

However, sadly, even though Father got much better in just a week and was stable, his doctor, Tang Xiao Yong, didn't allow him to check out of the hospital. Three weeks after Father was admitted to Chongqing Emergency Hospital, he was cross-infected with pneumonia. Father became frail and thin. When doctor Chen Rong prescribed him a 100 ml, 20g Human Serum Albumin (HSA) injection on October 31st, I thought it was some kind of nourishing treatment and agreed, even though I didn't have the money for it. Father's insurance didn't cover the cost[8], so I had to sell my part of our beach house in Baja, California, to my ex-husband at a loss to get the money.

Perhaps the dosage of the treatment was too much for Father. On November 2nd, 2022, he developed a gastric ulcer, and his stomach started bleeding. When I heard this bad news, I was really concerned, and through a friend's help, I managed to get in touch with Vice President Guo of the hospital. He went to see my father immediately and arranged for him to be moved to the main Intensive Care Unit of the hospital. I didn't know that Vice President Guo had just helped Father avoid a fatal disaster until later.

Each department in the hospital has its own ICU. My father was originally in the Neurosurgery

---

[8] Usually, doctors in China may receive commissions from prescribing self-paid medicines. So, they are incentivized to overdose.

Department. His doctor, Tang Xiao Yong, was attempting to transfer him to the department ICU before the vice president arrived to intervene. On the same day, doctor Tang made my brother Rong buy 300 ml of HSA and planned to keep the same dosage as before.

In the main ICU, Father's new doctor suggested a procedure to install a ventilator on his trachea. Father, however, vehemently resisted this proposal. The doctor, seeing the anguish in his eyes and feeling the weight of the decision, made the compassionate choice to permit my brother, Rong, to enter the tightly controlled ICU area.

My first instinct was to reject the ventilator, but Rong accused me of not being a doctor. He suggested that we should listen to the professionals. So, I hesitantly allowed him to push for Father's cooperation with the doctor.

As Rong entered the room, Father urgently shared his rejection of the ventilator, believing that those present wanted to 'kill him.' With genuine concern, my second brother reassured him,

"Papa, don't be afraid. These are friends of Jin Lan, who loves you more than anyone else. They're here to help you, to make things better. Please, trust in them."

Upon hearing these words, tears welled up in Father's eyes and began to trickle down his cheeks. It was a heart-wrenching sight described by Rong. Overwhelmed with a sense of helplessness, Father lost hope. Despite our well-intentioned efforts, we were often unaware of the depth of his pain and the wisdom he naturally possessed[9]. Eventually, with my consent, Rong signed the agreement for Father's surgery, which would involve installing the ventilator. It was a difficult decision made with the hope of improving Father's condition and providing him with the care he needed.

Knowing Father will be installed on a ventilator soon, I devoted an entire day to immersing myself in research, delving into cases involving ventilator applications from the perspective of medical

---

[9] The traditional wisdom of the Chinese is that Mother Nature has the function to heal everything, medicine/surgery just relieve the symptoms temporarily to win time for self-healing.

professionals. Every article I absorbed seemed to describe a distressing pattern: patients often developed a delusion that their doctors were murdering them. This insight made me believe that Father might be caught in the throes of a similar delusion.

Then my heart ached as I replayed the conversation in my mind – on the third day of his hospital stay, Father told Rong on the phone,

"Rong, please come to save me quickly; these people are harming me," because Father loudly requested to check out the hospital every day and night, his doctor prescribed high dosages of medicine to put him to oversleep. Of course, we didn't know this fact until two months later when we got to see Father's medical records.

When Rong shared this information with me, he thought it was funny because of the belief that hospitals only have angels. I also struggled to take Father's words seriously because, after all, he was 91 years old. Society often carries the misconception that elderly individuals may experience cognitive decline, which can lead to misunderstandings and misinterpretations of their words and actions. It was a moment when we unintentionally dismissed the

THE JOURNEY TO AWAKENING 23

possibility of something more profound underlying Father's distressing statements.

That very night, my heart raced, and sleep eluded me. I urgently texted Rong, pouring out my fears:

"Listen, I need to share something, but promise me you won't tell a soul. Just stay vigilant. I've got this gut feeling that maybe, just maybe, Father's concerns about some people wanting to harm him might be legit. So, please, keep a close eye on him, okay?"

My message was a plea, a silent scream of worry for Father's well-being that I entrusted only to my brother's ears.

Even though Rong didn't sense anything amiss, I remained insistent. I urged him to head to the hospital and retract the authorization for the ventilator surgery. Following this, I took it upon myself to contact the doctor, conveying my firm stance: "I want you to strictly employ the best and the most conservative treatments to aid my father."

Despite her warning that Father's life might be at risk without the ventilator, she eventually conceded to my plea, understanding the importance of preserving his dignity during his final days. In response, she arranged for a massage therapist to attend to my father daily. I asked her whether I needed to buy more Human Serum Albumin for Father, and she responded,

"No, no need, his stomach is still bleeding; we can only give him a very small dosage per day; too much will be harmful to him."

The next day, I immersed myself in a series of articles written from the perspective of survivors who had been through the ventilator applications. Every single one of them expressed that if they were faced with the choice again between the ventilator and death, they would opt for the latter. Reading these accounts, I felt an overwhelming sense of relief wash over me. It became abundantly clear that our decision to withdraw the authorization had been the right one, ensuring that Father wouldn't have to endure an unnecessarily difficult path in his final moments.

On that very day, I stumbled upon a Buddhist mantra known as Avalokitesvara bodhisattva's *"Six-*

Character Great Bright Mantra[10]," which goes, "Om Mani Padme Hum." I began to recite it faithfully, both day and night, in the hope that it might alleviate Father's suffering. Although I couldn't fully comprehend why or how this mantra was believed to work, my heart was filled with genuine hope that it could bring relief to Father during this challenging time.

On November 10th, 2022, Father's condition significantly improved; his stomach stopped bleeding for three days, and he felt stronger. So, he was moved from the main ICU to the regular patient area. Rong was granted permission to accompany Father in the hospital, which was a comforting development. On this very day, amidst all the emotions and challenges, Ken and I also had our official wedding ceremony at the city hall in Brooklyn, New York.

The very next morning, on November 11th, I found myself on the way back to Chongqing, China, where my parents resided. It was a journey filled with mixed feelings, leaving behind the joy of our wedding day in New York and returning to my family's

---

[10] https://en.wikipedia.org/wiki/Om_mani_padme_hum

side in China during what had been such a trying period.

***

After going through a complex series of PCR tests and enduring a four-day quarantine in Hong Kong, I finally arrived in Chongqing. The atmosphere was palpably tense due to the ongoing pandemic, and preventive measures were in full swing. Sterilization efforts seemed constant, with everything receiving regular cleaning with disinfectant. People on duty were outfitted in protective gear that made them look like participants in a battle against the virus; they were often referred to as the "Big Whites" on social media.

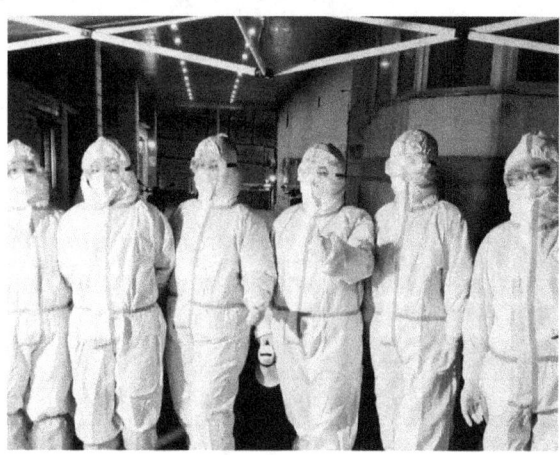

Upon arrival, I was checked into Yi Ke Sha Hotel, a quarantine hotel, for an additional four days. This was a necessary step before I could return to my home, where I would continue to undergo two more weeks of quarantine. The whole experience was a stark reminder of the widespread impact of the pandemic and the heightened precautions that had become a part of daily life. During my four-day stay at the quarantine hotel, the staff members were incredibly polite and attentive, going out of their way to meet our needs and ensure our comfort.

Then Rong said he was frightened when he saw Father loudly and repeatedly shouting my mother's name into the air every night. Although I initially believed that Father might be talking in his sleep, Rong revealed that he was, in fact, fully awake during these episodes. I thought Father must have missed Mother so much.

Mysteriously, on that night, although YouTube was banned in China and my VPN[11] was

---

[11] https://azure.microsoft.com/en-us/resources/cloud-computing-dictionary/what-is-

disabled, it unexpectedly presented me with a few videos. One was a Tedtalk lecture by Nanci Trivellato [12] discussing *How Out of Body Experiences Could Transform Yourself and the Society*, followed by a lecture on *The Surprising Benefits of Astral Projection*[13] by Mind Valley. I felt strange because I hadn't actively searched for anything related to these topics.

Prior to watching these videos, I had no inkling that such phenomena even existed, and I couldn't fathom how they might be connected to my own life. I simply ignored them and focused on the details of helping Father and Mother. I had so many challenges ahead of me.

Upon completing my four days of quarantine at the hotel, the government arranged for a car to take

---

vpn#:~:text=A%20VPN%2C%20which%20stands%20for,and%20firewalls%20on%20the%20internet.

[12] https://youtu.be/NMBNZ-spmn7I?si=S3NXnUOjPzmhWDgQ

[13] https://youtu.be/gaMeQxH5Mh4?si=pYqod-BvltvzyFxmk

me home. It's amazing that this giant city of 31 million was so organized to such details. During the ride, I struck up a conversation with the driver and shared with him that my father was currently in the hospital, emphasizing the need for all the prayers and positive thoughts we could muster. The driver turned out to be incredibly kind.

He mentioned his friend, Yu Mei, who happened to be a devout Christian and known for her powerful prayers. Before dropping me off at my gate, he thoughtfully connected us on WeChat. It was a heartwarming gesture, knowing that there were people out there willing to offer their support and spiritual guidance during such challenging moments.

After I retrieved my luggage from the elevator, someone locked it and informed me that I was not allowed to leave the building for the next two weeks. Even if I could walk down the stairs, I could not escape the two layers of locked and guarded gates of our building and the community. I acknowledged their instructions, understanding the importance of adhering to quarantine protocols.

Upon reaching my mom and eldest brother Li, who had been looking after her, I could see the excitement in my mom's eyes. She eagerly anticipated sharing some peculiar incidents that had occurred to her.

"Last week, something unusual happened every night," my mom shared, her eyes filled with curiosity.

"A man came into my room and sat by my bedside. Strangely, he wouldn't say a word. I repeatedly asked him why he wouldn't talk since he was right there, but he simply refused to respond." Her voice held a sense of wonder and confusion as she described such puzzling nightly visits.

Reminded by those lectures about Out of Body Experiences on YouTube, it struck me that the man my mom described might be Father's spirit. However, I refrained from discussing this with Mom because, in Chinese tradition, there's a belief that before passing away, individuals could have godly functions – 通天[14]. I hesitated to accept the possibility that Father might be nearing the end of his life; I just

---

[14] https://cibei.org.my/postdm119

wasn't emotionally prepared for that reality, and I believed that his health had no serious illness. Especially my classmate Luo Cao, who is a famous doctor in Chongqing, checked my father's medical record and told me that my father needed nothing special but nutrition.

During the daytime, I assumed my eldest brother's responsibilities, which primarily involved tending to all of Mom's needs. In the evenings, I embarked on a new journey of learning how to pray, guided by the wise and compassionate Christian woman, Yu Mei. I dedicated my prayers to Father, fervently imploring for his recovery. In the name of Jesus Christ, I prayed for Father's body to experience complete healing, pouring my heart and faith into these words of hope and love.

I confided in Yu Mei, expressing my genuine desire to believe in Jesus Christ and my struggle to comprehend how prayers truly worked. I admitted that my prayers, though sincere, lacked confidence. In response, Yu Mei offered comforting words, assuring me that it was all right and that the power of prayer came from Jesus himself. She explained that we essentially borrowing that power from him.

Encouraged by her wisdom and kindness, I began to incorporate both Christian prayers and the Buddhist mantra into my daily and nightly rituals, all dedicated to Father's well-being. It was a heartfelt blend of faiths, driven by a deep desire to provide comfort and healing for my beloved Father.

Then Doctor Tang prescribed 100 ml of Human Serum Albumin[15] (HSA) @20 grams per day for a total of six days for Father, which made me panic again. I had read two expert articles highlighting the potential negative effects of HSA, including the risk of organ failure and other complications. Oddly, when I attempted to find the same sources on Google to reference in my book, I couldn't locate a single piece of related information. However, I did manage to find a few professional sources on Baidu.com and took a screenshot of one of them as evidence.

---

[15] Negative effects of Human Serum Albumin:
https://assets-dam.takeda.com/raw/upload/v1675870083/legacy-dotcom/siteassets/zh-cn/home/what-we-do/our-products/_200x50ml_vienna_s20160018_20200901.pdf

It was a perplexing situation, and I felt a heightened sense of responsibility to ensure Father's well-being amidst the uncertainty surrounding his treatment.

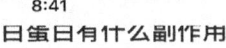

Negative Impacts of Human Serum Albumin

As per the insights of a reputable pharmacist, Dr Wang Hai Lian, affiliated with China's Capital Medical University, Human Serum Albumin (HSA) could potentially lead to a range of adverse reactions. These may include anaphylactic shock, hypersensitivity reactions, as well as laryngeal edema, bronchial asthma, and breathing difficulties. Additionally, HSA might be associated with more severe complications like heart failure, pulmonary edema, myocardial infarction, and various cardiac arrhythmias, including atrial fibrillation, tachycardia, or bradycardia. These insights shed light on the complexities and risks associated with HSA treatment, adding to the concerns about Father's well-being during his medical journey.

Furthermore, HSA treatment can cause various problems. It can affect the body in different ways, both physically and mentally. It might change the patient's blood pressure, making it too high or too low. Sometimes, it can make a patient feel restless, hyperactive, or even a bit manic. There could be issues with the stomach, like bleeding, feeling sick, or throwing up. The liver might also be affected. In some cases, it can cause problems with the kidneys, leading to lower back pain or even damage. A patient might experience strange feelings in the body, like

THE JOURNEY TO AWAKENING 35

dizziness, headaches, or changes in how things taste. There can also be skin problems, like hives or rashes, and sometimes, the patient might get feverish or chilly.

These possible side effects show that HSA treatment is quite complex and may not be the best choice in certain situations, such as Father's. It's crucial to keep a close watch on the dosages and the necessities of using it. In Father's case, he never needed it; his protein index always stayed above the reference number.

Before Father received the HSA injections, he had never experienced any of the symptoms mentioned above throughout his entire life. However, when I visited him in the hospital, he was dealing with 10+ of these symptoms. It was heartbreaking to witness his deteriorating condition. What made the situation even more difficult was that Doctor Tang seemed to keep important information from us. He consistently reassured us that Father was getting better each day despite the stark reality that HSA was killing him again every day.

My heart felt that something was seriously amiss, and my anxiety was through the roof. I called Doctor Tang every day, fervently urging him to reconsider the dosage and sharing what I had read about HSA. Sadly, he seemed indifferent to my concerns, brushing me aside. Every day, I pleaded with him to let me stay with Father, hoping to provide the comfort and support he needed. Finally, on December 4th, Doctor Tang relented, and by December 5th, 2022, I had moved in because the hospital requested a PCR test in 24 hours.

***

Surprisingly, when I arrived at the hospital, Doctor Tang, who oversaw my father's case for over one month, didn't want to meet me in person, although he was next door. He was hidden from me all the time. I never got to see him, although I had sent four indirect friends, who were his colleagues in the hospital, to beg him to take good care of Father.

As they wheeled Father in from the Department ICU, where a tube had been inserted into his trachea, my heart ached at the sight of his frailty. He looked so thin but not weak. The moment was heavy with emotion, and then the nursing aid cried out, "Look, he has black stool."

My gut told me that Father was experiencing stomach bleeding again. I was angry that Doctor Tang had never mentioned this and continued to administer large doses of HSA injections for so long. I didn't voice it because the **Law of Attraction** suggests that I should focus on the positive things that I could do. So, I immediately jumped in to do whatever I could to ease Father's suffering and make him feel better.

Father was noticeably cold and shivering, so I asked him if he needed a blanket. He nodded eagerly, without hesitation. I covered him with the blanket I had brought for myself. After the nurses had finished their tasks and left, I began to gently rub Father's icy-cold feet until they gradually warmed up.

The wife of the patient in the neighboring bed observed the scene and said to her husband, "You see, only a daughter can be so close to her father. You are fortunate we have a daughter." Father couldn't speak due to the tube in his throat, but his grip on my hand spoke volumes. It was a silent but profound connection, affirming the depth of our bond.

The hospital staff would frequently enter Father's room, causing his frail body to tremble with discomfort. Each time the nurse departed, I swiftly approached Father, grasping his arm firmly with both hands. With closed eyes, I began to chant Avalokitesvara bodhisattva's *Six-Character Great and Bright Mantra*, "Om Mani Padme Hum..."

In a matter of about two minutes, Father's trembling would gradually subside. Remarkably, it seemed to work every time, even though I couldn't fully comprehend why or how. It was as though the power of those sacred words provided solace and relief to Father's suffering body even though he couldn't understand what I was chanting.

Even though sharing a room with eight people felt chaotic, I was content because I could be by my father's side. I was grateful that I had a foldable chair to sleep on during the night. My hope remained steadfast; I clung to the belief that Father would eventually recover and return home with me. After all, I knew he had been in good health prior to this sudden and troubling incident.

On the second day, Father's condition took a turn for the worse as he developed a high fever. A nurse had to remove all the food from his stomach, and it was evident that there was blood in the extracted contents. This starkly confirmed the initial gut feeling I had the moment I saw Father. My emotions welled up, and I was overwhelmed with anger and frustration at the situation.

Subsequently, the attending doctor summoned me to his office, and the words he spoke were like a devastating blow to my heart. He told me to prepare myself for the inevitable - that Father's time with us was ending. I couldn't bring myself to accept this grim conclusion.

After all, when Father entered the hospital, he had no life-threatening conditions. I even have a video of him taken on the seventh day of his hospitalization, where he appeared perfectly fine. Moreover, none of the medical reports hinted at any significant issues, and his head injury healed.

What made the situation even more agonizing was Father's unwavering desire to leave the hospital, a wish he had expressed daily since the 3rd day of his admission. Brother Rong visited the hospital daily, advocating for Father's release, but our pleas fell on deaf ears. The frustration and despair in those moments were indescribable as I grappled with the profound injustice of it all.

In the evening, I sat by Father's bedside and showed him a video of Mom talking to him. He watched it with great attention, and I held his arm with both of my hands. I said my prayers in the name of Jesus Christ, followed by chanting Avalokitesvara bodhisattva's *Six-Character Great Bright Mantra*, "Om Mani Padme Hum, Om Mani Padme Hum..." My heart still clung to the hope that perhaps, against all odds, a miracle could occur.

On December 8th, 2022, a liver specialist came to examine Father and inquired about any history of his liver issues. I replied that my father had always been exceptionally healthy and had no such history. However, in the afternoon, the on-call doctor, Chen Rong, summoned me to his office once again. He gravely informed me that Father's time was near, and he would likely pass away that night.

Hearing those words, I felt utterly shattered and couldn't contain my anger, "Why is he dying? He was perfectly fine on the 7th day of hospitalization."

Doctor Chen asked, "What evidence do you have that he was fine?"

Me, "I have a video of him on the seventh day of his hospitalization. He appeared to be healthy and energized. Even though he repeatedly and loudly expressed a strong desire to go home, Doctor Tang insisted on keeping him in the hospital, and that resulted in his contraction of pneumonia."

"Then you overdosed Human Serum Albumin, which resulted in his gastric ulcer and stomach bleeding, and he was checked in the main ICU."

Doctor Chen seemed taken aback and retorted, "How can you claim that HSA caused his gastric ulcer?"

I replied firmly, "I conducted thorough research. Moreover, the doctor in the main ICU clearly stated that the HSA dosage had to be lowered to half of what he got; otherwise, it would be harmful to Father. Once the dosage was reduced, Father's stomach bleeding stopped in four days. This improvement was the reason he was transferred out of the main ICU."

Doctor Chen looked at me with a regretful expression and confessed,

"There is something seriously wrong with his blood. We are neurosurgery experts, not blood specialists. We have no knowledge of prescribing medicine for blood; we made a grave mistake."

He then displayed a figure from Father's blood test on his computer screen: *Aspartate Aminotransferase*[16], with a staggering reading of *765*. This revelation felt like an explosion in my head, as this number should typically fall between 15 and 40. When it had initially reached 152, I had already bombarded Doctor Tang, when he prescribed Father the high dosages of HSA, with a barrage of phone calls and text messages trying to stop him.

The staggering number of 765 was a drastic departure from the normal range, shattering my faith in the efficacy of my prayers to alter Father's critical condition. At that time, I still lacked a proper

---

[16] https://en.wikipedia.org/wiki/Aspartate_transaminase

understanding of how prayers could work. A month later, after Father had already passed away, I would gain clarity on this matter. However, at that moment, I felt defeated and relinquished any hope of influencing Father's fate through my prayers. I made the difficult decision to prioritize Father's comfort and told Doctor Chen that I wanted his final moments to be free from pain.

Father was enduring immense suffering, yet he was unable to articulate his pain due to the tracheal tube. Reflecting on this later, I realized the gravity of the decision I had made for Father. I allowed this situation to unfold, and the weight of that choice has haunted me ever since. It was a decision I can never forgive myself for.

Following this, Doctor Chen prescribed painkillers for Father. A nurse explained what to anticipate for the upcoming night. I walked back to Father's bedside in a daze, devoid of strength to utter a single word or even summon my brothers.

That evening, Father peacefully drifted into slumber under the influence of painkillers. I sat by his side, grasping his arm with both hands as I had done before, and chanted Avalokitesvara bodhisattva's *Six-Character Great Bright Mantra*, "Om Mani Padme Hum..." until exhaustion overtook me in the darkness, and I fell asleep.

My sleep was disrupted by the warning machine around 4 am, indicating that Father had stopped breathing while his heart still beat. I swiftly pressed the red button, summoning Doctor Chen, and nurses. They observed him until his heart ceased its rhythmic beat entirely. At that point, they moved to remove the medical apparatus attached to his body, but I halted their actions, preventing them from breaking Father's peace.

Doctor Chen granted me a mere 30 minutes for humanitarian reasons, emphasizing that they would need to relocate Father's body to the morgue afterwards. My heart was heavy with sorrow, and I lacked the strength to notice my brothers immediately. It felt as though my world was collapsing around me.

In that dark room, I remained seated, clutching Father's still-warm arm with both of my hands. I closed my eyes and continued to chant Avalokitesvara bodhisattva's *Six-Character Great*

Bright Mantra, "Om Mani Padme Hum..." until Doctor Chen and the nurses returned to remove everything from Father's body and escort me out.

Once they had completed their duties, I addressed Doctor Chen with grief and determination, "I want all the records detailing my father's hospital experience."

"They are kept in the Medical Record Department," he replied. "It may take about a week for you to receive them all." Despite the immense pain and loss, I knew that obtaining those records was crucial to understanding what had transpired during Father's hospitalization.

After the medical team departed, the room remained enveloped in darkness. I hesitated to awaken the others who were sleeping, particularly because I wanted to preserve the tranquility around Father. He had just emerged from the harrowing nightmare of nearly two months, and I wanted him to find his peace.

With a quiet demeanor, I gathered my belongings and made my way to the staircase. I informed my brothers about Father's passing. My second brother, Rong, upon hearing the tragic news, swiftly set off for the hospital. Simultaneously, my eldest brother Li learned of the situation and assured us he would return soon despite being out of town now.

When I returned to Father's sick room, my heart sank at the sight of the hospital workers having already placed him in a somber yellow body bag. The situation was grim, and it was one of the most awful sights I had ever seen. One of the workmen motioned for me to follow him as he carried Father's body to a special lift that would lower us to the mortuary in the garage level. I followed him in the darkness. My feet were heavy, and the weight of the situation was pressing down on me like a leaden load.

The garage was super dark and cold. There was no heat; the air was incredibly chilly. The rows of cold storage freezers at the mortuary gave off a particularly chilly feeling. Strangers' dead bodies surrounded me as I stood in the poorly illuminated mortuary, a melancholy reminder of the unrelenting toll the Covid-19 pandemic had taken.

Despite my ingrained phobia of the dark and the dead, I was surprised I stayed calm and firm. It felt as though I was stronger than the great pain. I knew I could finish this arduous journey.

Later, Brother Rong arrived and took me back home. Brother Li had also returned by then. We made a difficult decision not to share this devastating news with our mother. We knew that if she were to learn of Father's passing, it could utterly shatter her and extinguish her will to carry on. She had been immensely spoiled by Father's love and care throughout their life, and the thought of her trying to navigate this world without him was unfathomable. We couldn't bear the idea of losing both of our parents simultaneously.

***

We arranged an altar in my living room[17], and each of us lighted incense sticks and candles that burned for seven days and nights. Whenever I lit those incense sticks in honor of Father, my emotions overwhelmed me. The weight of the decisions I had made, which seemed to contribute to Father's

---

[17] My parents were living in my home in Chongqing, China.

suffering and eventual passing…I could never forgive myself. During these moments, I would chant Avalokitesvara bodhisattva's *Six-Character Great Bright Mantra*, "Om Mani Padme Hum…" for about 15 minutes each time. The mantra held a mysterious comfort, even though I still didn't grasp its meaning or workings. I simply knew that many believed it was beneficial for the recently departed.

The loss of our beloved father was a profound ache, amplified by the knowledge that mistakes could have been averted had we not placed so much trust in those we considered experts. Fueled by this sense of injustice, we engaged a legal firm to pursue a lawsuit against the hospital and the responsible doctor. It was clear that Doctor Tang Xiao Yong had misused his authority and betrayed the trust we had placed in him. During our attempts to access Father's medical records, Doctor Tang even sent someone to plead for negotiation, but I firmly declined.

On another occasion, when Rong attempted to settle the bill at the hospital's cashier, he was informed that payment would not be accepted unless he spoke with Doctor Tang. In response, I advised him not to proceed with the payment at that moment. After I left China, the hospital reached out to Rong and informed him that they had covered the outstanding bills on our behalf. Despite this, my anger and inability to forgive both Doctor Tang and myself persisted. As a result, the lawsuit against the hospital and the responsible doctor continues to this day.

I thought I could never forgive Doctor Tang, who cold-bloodedly killed my father for money and let my father suffer such great pains that he didn't deserve. I didn't know that the deeper meaning of pain was showing me the path to enlightenment until everything started to unfold. The pain of losing Father and the pain of observing his pains guided me to the path that I never thought I would step on.

Striking Life Science Experiments:

A Web of Stars

"Everything is a conscious existence."

-Thales of Miletus

While I was searching for the answer to where my father was gone, the Universe blinked a path decorated with a web of extraordinarily brilliant stars that bridged ancient wisdom and modern science. Through them, I found Father and my True Self, the most valuable treasure and meaning of life.

When the lockdown restrictions finally lifted, I hired a full-time caregiver, along with my eldest brother Li, to take care of Mom. This arrangement allowed me to worry less about her while I continued to accompany Father in the hospital. However, after Father's passing, nearly everyone around me seemed to contract infections, though fortunately, none of the cases were severe. Then, almost as mysteriously as it had arrived, the virus seemed to vanish, and life gradually returned to normal.

During this time, a flood of videos began appearing on my YouTube[18] feed. They weren't new topics, but their unique perspectives and credible sources impressed me. They helped me understand not only why and how prayers work but also who I am. I finally realized that some of the incredible miracles described in religious texts like *The Bible*, the Buddhist Sutras, and in some ancient Chinese literature works such as *Pilgrimage to the West*[19] were not merely fanciful tales but could be profoundly true human experiences.

---

[18] Although Youtube is banned in China, I could access it with a VPN.

[19] https://en.wikipedia.org/wiki/Journey_to_the_West

As I absorbed this newfound knowledge, I couldn't help but feel a mix of wonder and awe. It was as though a veil had been lifted, revealing a profound understanding of the Universe and life. This revelation brought both solace and a renewed sense of curiosity to my heart.

*** Star 1 ***

Among the web of those extraordinarily brilliant stars, one of them is Xiao Cui, who dived into the fascinating world of Qi Gong in a YouTube video[20]. Despite looking like he was barely out of his teens, Xiao Cui spoke with the wisdom of a sage who had seen thousand years of life. His talk was nothing short of impressiveness. He took us on a profound journey through the essence and history of Qi Gong, revealing the hidden depths of this ancient practice.

---

[20] https://www.youtube.com/watch?v=FweM2Hld7Yk

THE JOURNEY TO AWAKENING 53

硬核解析修行的真相！原來冥想打坐禪修丹道都是練氣功！｜塔哥奇談

Xiao Cui summarized, based on the concept that the Universe is one conscious life, Qi Gong is a practice that improves or perfects the functions of the human body and turns usual ability into self-aware intelligence through active, introverted exercise of conscious activities.

But what really got my neurons firing was when Xiao Cui dropped a bombshell: *practicing Qi Gong was essentially practicing meditation.* My interest was piqued because it connected the dots between meditation and prayers. I knew that we could heal ourselves by meditation, but Qi Gong can heal others without even touching the patients or from thousands of miles away. I was curious to see how he could explain that scientifically.

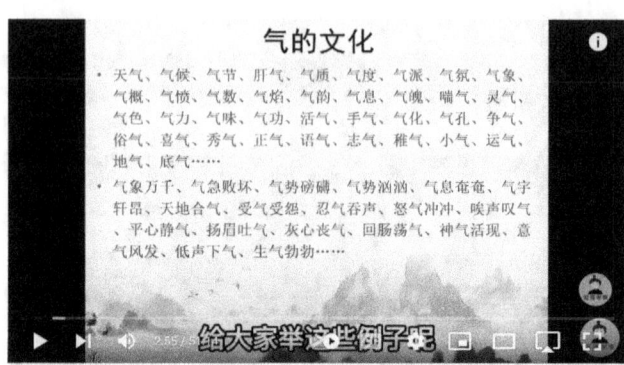

Xiao Cui Listed How the Word Qi is Used in Every Respect of Our Lives in Chinese

** Star 2 **

So, I delved further into this intriguing topic. I watched another video featuring Xiao Cui, this time interviewing Xia Min Hong[21], a young researcher in the field of life science in Qi Gong. The discussion revolved around the remarkable notion of using Qi Gong to heal broken chicken bones. Yes, you read that correctly: chicken bones. It sounded like something out of a bizarre science fiction story, and I

---

[21] https://www.youtube.com/watch?v=dt41UDa1U8g

THE JOURNEY TO AWAKENING

couldn't wait to hear how they were making sense of it.

專訪90後氣功科研人員，意識真能影響物質？披露不可思議的超自然實驗！| 塔哥奇

During the interview, Mr. Xia, the young researcher, shared his remarkable journey. He came from a lineage of lifelong Qi Gong practitioners, with his father, grandfather, and great-grandfather all steeped in this ancient art. However, he had never been particularly interested in Qi Gong until 2015, when his father asked for his help with training in my hometown, Chongqing. Reluctantly, he embarked on this journey and spent 15 months learning the foundations of Qi Gong. Little did he know that this experience would open the door to an entirely new world, one that would forever change how he saw the world around him.

With newfound enthusiasm, Mr. Xia sought to make a significant impact but couldn't find the right opportunity. Three days before the Spring Festival of 2016, a friend Mr. Xia had made during his time in Chongqing called him. He informed Mr. Xia that their research branch in Xi An was recruiting elite Qi Gong experts for some groundbreaking scientific experiments. This news filled him with excitement, but he hesitated, believing he wasn't qualified. The research team seemed to be seeking highly renowned professors exclusively, while he held only an undergraduate degree.

Yet, Mr. Xia's determination prevailed. With a heart full of enthusiasm, he picked up the phone and dialled the recruiter's number. He shared his family's rich history of Qi Gong practice, his voice resonating with excitement and passion. To his astonishment, the recruiter's response was a positive one: "Sounds great, please come and join us." The words hit him like a bolt of lightning, reigniting his impatience. He was eager to board a flight from Shenyang, where his entire family was gathering from different parts of the country for their annual reunion.

THE JOURNEY TO AWAKENING 57

Finally, in early 2016, Mr. Xia's journey led him to the research team in Xi An. He was placed directly in the Chicken Bone Healing project, a remarkable endeavor. The team's mission involved conducting over 100 experiments aimed at healing broken chicken bones using the collective power of Qi Gong practitioners. For 18 months, they tirelessly delved into this extraordinary venture.

Mr. Xia's team faced certain challenges in their research. Due to strict academic standards, they included only 82 cases in their thesis. Remarkably, out of these 82 cases, 67 displayed significant results.

專訪90後氣功科研人員，意識真能影響物質？披露不可思議的超自然實驗！｜塔哥奇

The Research Team's Thesis on Chicken Bone Healing with Qi Qong

Significant results in this context meant that these chicken bones had fully recovered in a mere 12 hours. To put this into perspective, according to the president of the College of Animal Studies, mentioned by Mr. Xia, a chicken typically takes 3-4 weeks to form a poroma, another 4-5 weeks to heal the bone, and 1-2 years to completely recover to the point where the poroma disappears. In the best-case scenario observed by Mr. Xia's team, it took an astonishingly brief 2 minutes and 17 seconds for a broken bone to heal completely, leaving no trace of the prior fracture.

Unfortunately, this rapid healing occurred so swiftly that his team couldn't capture all the necessary X-ray images during the process. Instead, they cited a case that took 6 minutes and was thoroughly documented.

Mr. Xia also discussed how Qi Gong practitioners employ the power of the mind to influence a local structure of spacetime, effectively closing gaps in broken bones or eliminating tumor cells. He encouraged individuals who aren't Qi Gong practitioners to conduct simple experiments, such as using the power of their minds to bridge pieces of a sliced cucumber[22]. These endeavors shed light on the concept that thoughts can have impacts on the physical world.

專訪90後氣功科研人員，意識真能影響物質？披露不可思議的超自然實驗！|

---

[22] In Qi Gong, there are seven principle command messages: 开合出入聚散化 - open, merge, out, enter, gather, dismiss, disappear. That means, you can use your mind to order anything to disappear or appear, because the building blocks of the Universe is the same, the only differences are the forms which can be changed according to our mind.

https://idea.cas.cn/viewdoc.action?docid=76574

專訪90後氣功科研人員，意識真能影響物質？披露不可思議的超自然實驗！|

Through his hard work and deep thinking, Mr. Xia realized that China's precious cultural heritage, the concept of harmonious integration of the human body and the universe (expressed as 天人合一), isn't just an ideal goal. *Instead, oneness is an objective reality that no one can escape.* All existences in the universe, from the micro to the macro, are just different levels of density and forms of structured Qi, which is a conscious being that can communicate directly to anything by synchronicity of light waves (image)/sound waves.

Mr. Xia also noticed that the influence of consciousness operates faster than the speed of light, which is why most people can't imagine that the effects could be true. Naturally, Qi Gong practitioners with various levels of compassion/sensitivity have different levels of power. The more refined their sensitivity/compassion[23] is, the more extraordinary feats they can achieve.

Mr. Xia encouraged people to explore the depths of our *Original Self*[24] more profoundly. He believes that just as a young sapling's mission is to manifest a magnificent tree or forest by growing deep roots, a human being's life mission should be to unlock and manifest the incredible functions gifted by the Universe for noble purposes. It would be deeply regretful if we never get to know our greatest gift while our life is gone. What an exceptional young man! I'm truly proud of him. I was never so deep even though I lived 56 years of life.

And you know what? I've come to realize that when a Qi Gong master broke a piece of stone with his hand, it was not because his hand was exceptionally powerful. Instead, it was because his

---

[23] Refined sensibility here means very kind, pure, tolerate and compassionate heart.

[24] By this time, I had no idea what *Original Self/True Self* means. I heard the word, *"higher self"*, didn't understand what that means either.

mind communicated with the stone, and the stone willingly altered its spacetime structure (loosened the bonds between the molecules), allowed him to break the stone effortlessly. While we, as the audiences, focused on the belief that it was a piece of hard stone, it had already altered itself as a pile of sand. It's akin to a nurse asking you to relax your muscles before giving you a shot – your mind agrees to let the spacetime structure of your muscle loosen, making the shot possible.

I've finally grasped how prayers function. They act as directives from the mind, and everything in the Universe communicates by the synchronicities of sound waves and light waves (images). Prayers can swiftly alter the targeted local structure of spacetime on physical, biological, and chemical levels. Why? Because we aren't isolated individuals, we're all interconnected within the fabric of spacetime as a single conscious entity, the source of the Universe [25]. That's why Einstein's Special

---

[25] Also, the fact that Zero-point energy is constantly dynamic and uncertain could be the best hint of what the universe is and why we all matter to each other.

https://en.wikipedia.org/wiki/Zero-point_energy

Relativity theory exposed to us that the speed of light is the same to all observers within the Universe, no matter whether you are running toward or against the source of light. *The absolute truth stays the same for all; the relative truth varies accordingly.*

Now, I have started to truly appreciate the wonder and magnificence of the Universe's original essence.

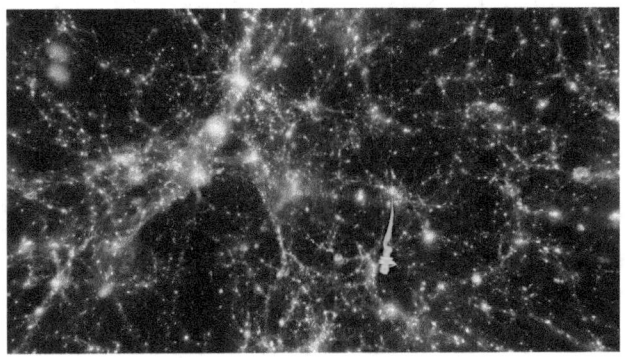

After obtaining this understanding, I frequently reflect on how having this knowledge earlier could have made a profound difference when my father was still with us. It's as though I missed out on a hidden power that could have allowed me to help Father more. We could have shared more precious time together, and he could have said goodbye to my mother and brothers before he left.

So, instead of praying for his whole body to completely heal, I should have targeted the *Aspartate aminotransferase* in Father's liver and asked those molecules to be dismissed with a clear and focused mind. It should have been the communication between my mind and the molecules, not between my mind and Father's whole body. So, I could win time and heal Father's body step by step because I was not a Qi Gong master, and my mind power was too limited.

** Star 3 **

Intrigued by Mr. Xia, I delved into the work of another remarkable life science researcher and Qi Gong practitioner, Ms. Sun Chu Lin[26], who possesses around 60 astonishing mental abilities capable of altering objects on physical, chemical, and biological levels.

26

https://zhuanlan.zhihu.com/p/613068338

Ms. Sun Chu Lin Sprouted A Peanut
with Her Mind Power

Ms. Sun Chu Lin[27] was born in Wuhan, China, in 1957. During the Cultural Revolution, she was sent to her Nanjing grandmother's house. When she helped her grandmother do farm work, she first discovered that she could see through the ground and found a jar filled with copper coins. In 1979, as a kindergarten teacher at the Wuhan Institute of Geology, she found that she could use her ears to recognize words and see through the human body.

---

[27] https://www.ictmhw.com/copy-of-7?lang=en

In 1981, Ms. Sun Chu Lin worked briefly in the General Hospital of the Chinese People's Liberation Army, giving patients perspectives with her extraordinary functions. In 1987, she was officially transferred to the Institute of Life Science at China Geology University, where Professor Shen Jin Chuan was conducting a full-scale experimental study of life science.

Professor Shen Jin Chuan and Ms. Sun Chulin collaborated for 18 years, from 1987 to 2005, to conduct studies on her extraordinary mind power. Eighteen years of experimental data on the psi phenomenon (note: psi is the pronunciation of the Greek letter, representing the unknown meaning, like the X in the popular movie "X Archive") provide conclusive evidence of the existence of extraordinary mental function.

Ms. Sun Chulin demonstrated extraordinary psi ability and launched an unknown energy information complex, which strongly influenced related objects and living bodies and produced various physical, chemical, and biological effects.

One of the many miraculous experiments that Ms. Sun did over 1000 times in different countries[28], according to herself in an interview, was using her mind power to make deep-fried peanuts return to life and then grow them into 1+ inch long sprouts in a few minutes[29].

In the same interview, she mentioned that she used the same concept of time reversal to cure a Japanese boy's brain cancer. She reversed the five-year-old boy back to his three-year-old body when he had no brain cancer. Her such experience demonstrated that not only consciousness can directly influence objects spacewise, but also time travel.

---

[28] https://youtu.be/1-snzy91VEI?si=_2Egp5UNHO_twRNM

[29] https://youtu.be/tpDeZekksfY?si=5IzrPRvf26E3PpPQ

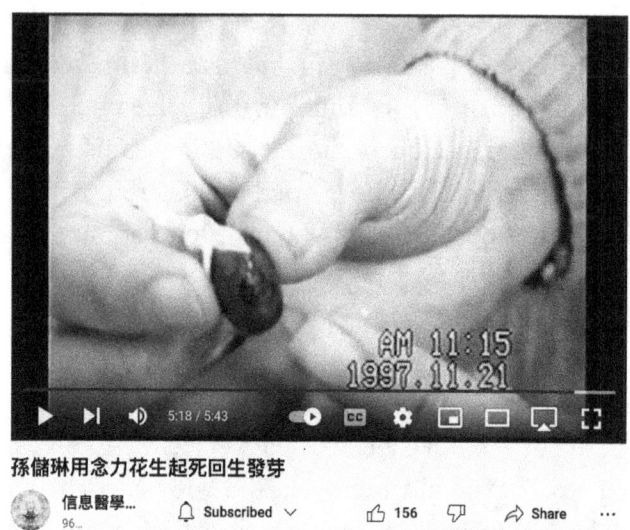

孫儲琳用念力花生起死回生發芽

In another experiment with the world-renowned Professor Shen Jin Chuan from the China University of Geoscience, Ms. Sun Chun Lin used her mind power to move the windmill inside a vacuumed Crookes Radiometer forward and backward from the next room.[30] The strange thing is that the windmill inside the vacuum was not supposed to be able to move backwards, but it did.

---

[30] https://youtu.be/kZsJhzcK-spE?si=_QisCGRNT5VGbbTx

THE JOURNEY TO AWAKENING

Not only was it moved backward, but it also messed up the clock connected to the device. When the windmill moved backward, the clock skipped 18 seconds to reach the next minute.

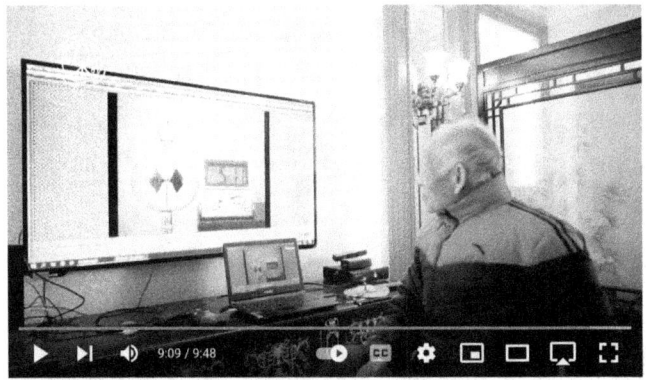

《时间都去哪了？》沈今川亲自破解"孙储琳意识光风车实验"

That means that one minute became 42 seconds instead of 60 seconds for the clock connected to the device. When the windmill was made to move forward, the clock became normal.

I then realized that antimatters could reverse time for the targeted matters. So, their information of spacetime structures cancels each other and then releases pure Qi/light. After all, everything is just an amount of Qi defined/captured by the information (order requested by higher conscious beings) of spacetime structure, such as molecular formulas. That's exciting!

There are also a few videos of Ms. Sun changing a bottle of water into a bottle of orange juice like something[31], moving a coin through a glass table[32], and some pictures taken by her mind without a camera[33]… I realized that the potential of our mind power is probably infinite. We just need to keep an open mind.

During the interviews, Ms. Sun Chu Lin presented as a remarkably genuine and sincere individual. She exuded a sense of humility and healed numerous people for free. It was evident that she approached her work as a life science researcher with the utmost seriousness and passion.

---

[31] https://youtu.be/ZwWd8hpdHoE?si=4Md-03NNlwVbtZpd

[32] https://youtu.be/wL11S6zf4-g?si=h5xDSz6OcwmDBGtt

[33] https://youtu.be/KEBdFA6L1Iw?si=eh84fuH-kJV7GlBSG

According to Dr. Yan Xin, who is a medical doctor and a grandmaster of Qi Gong[34], one must first demonstrate high moral ground to receive the profound insights given by Qi Gong grandmasters. It seems as if the high level of Qi Gong skill and integrity are necessary for the Universe to reveal its most profound mysteries. I found myself drawn into the fascinating world where science, spirituality, and personal ethics converged. It was a reminder of the profound connection between our humanity and the mysteries of Qi Gong.

** Star 4 **

After watching these impressive videos, I was so excited and told my husband, Ken, about the amazing achievements of Mr. Xia Hong Min and Ms. Sun Chu Lin. No matter how I presented him with the abundant scientific evidence from reputable universities in China, Ken would never believe a bit of it because he believes he is highly educated and well-read. If he never heard of it, it must not exist. Then,

---

[34] https://youtu.be/hdxnn-kjbvnE?si=zZSQD4Z4PmgyQCE0

an even more brilliant star twinkled on YouTube, that is, Dr. Yan Xin.

In the world of Qi Gong, where ancient practices and modern science meet, Dr. Yan Xin stands out. Among the grand Qi Gong masters today, Dr. Yan Xin is a pioneer with a unique mission. Since the 1980s, he has connected Eastern wisdom with Western science by carefully studying the mysterious functions of "Qi" in the academic laboratories of the top universities worldwide. In a CCTV interview in 1992, he said he had done 10,000+ scientific experiments with some of the world's top scientists.

As per the book I downloaded from CIA's website, *Yan Xin Qi Gong and the Contemporary Sciences*[35], by Jo Ann Wozniak and others, China's national TV station introduced Dr. Yan Xin held the position of a physician at the Chinese Traditional Medicine Research Institute in my hometown Chongqing, China, during the 1990s.

---

[35] https://www.cia.gov/readingroom/docs/CIA-RDP96-00792R000300430003-5.pdf

THE JOURNEY TO AWAKENING 73

Yan Xin @China's Embassy in the USA, in 2006

Prior to his study of Chinese traditional medicine, he pursued education in two Western medicine colleges in China. Dr. Yan Xin is a graduate of the University of Chinese Traditional Medicine in

Sichuan. He has five years of experience teaching Chinese traditional medicine.

Even as early as the 1990s, Dr. Yan Xin was actively involved in scientific research related to Chinese traditional medicine and the Chinese concept of Qi (pronounced Chee). Qi serves as the foundation for acupuncture, most martial arts styles, and the traditional Chinese understanding of both the human body and the universe. Dr. Yan Xin has already conducted numerous successful scientific studies in collaboration with prominent research institutes and universities, both within China and internationally. He also embarked on lecture tours, addressing audiences in the United States and the People's Republic of China.

By blending the principles of Chinese traditional medicine with the methodologies of Western medicine and harnessing the unique capabilities of high-level Qigong, Dr. Yan Xin has achieved remarkable success in treating a wide range of common and seemingly incurable illnesses. In some instances, the outcomes have appeared nothing short of miraculous and initially difficult to believe.

Dr. Yan Xin has rapidly healed patients with broken bones within minutes and, in some cases, provided relief to cancer patients within a few hours. He also successfully assisted an individual who had endured thirty years of deafness in regaining his hearing in a remarkably short period. Additionally, he administered Qi Gong treatment to an AIDS patient in Hong Kong, resulting in blood test results returning to normal by the third day of treatment, a condition that persisted even three years after the treatment was initiated.

In his quest to uncover the mysteries of Qi Gong, Dr. Yan Xin has engaged in collaborative endeavors with esteemed institutions like Beijing University, Tsinghua University, and the Chinese Academy of Sciences, along with various other scientific research organizations. The breadth of his experiments spans a wide spectrum of disciplines, encompassing Medicine, Biology, Physics, Nuclear Energy, Chemistry, Optics, Astronomy, Geology, Industry, and Agriculture. The outcomes of his research serve as compelling evidence that the inherent potential within every human being far surpasses the boundaries of contemporary scientific knowledge.

Dr. Yan Xin's research has yielded compelling evidence that a proficient Qi Gong master possesses the capacity to impact and alter the molecular composition of various test samples. This influence extends to substances like DNA and RNA, spanning distances ranging from 6 to 2000 kilometers. Additionally, it has been demonstrated that Qi Gong can also affect the half-life of radioactive isotopes and even manipulate the polarization plane of a beam of light generated by a Helium-Neon laser. These discoveries are reshaping the perspective of modern science and challenging long-held assumptions.

Up until 1991, Dr. Yan Xin had co-authored thirty-six scientific papers in collaboration with fellow scientists. Notably, some of the research findings have already been implemented in various industrial sectors within China.

In response to the high demand from individuals interested in Qi Gong and patients grappling with challenging ailments, Dr. Yan Xin delivered hundreds of Qi Gong presentations. These special lectures not only provided knowledge but also emitted Qi or energy to the audience, imparting healing effects.

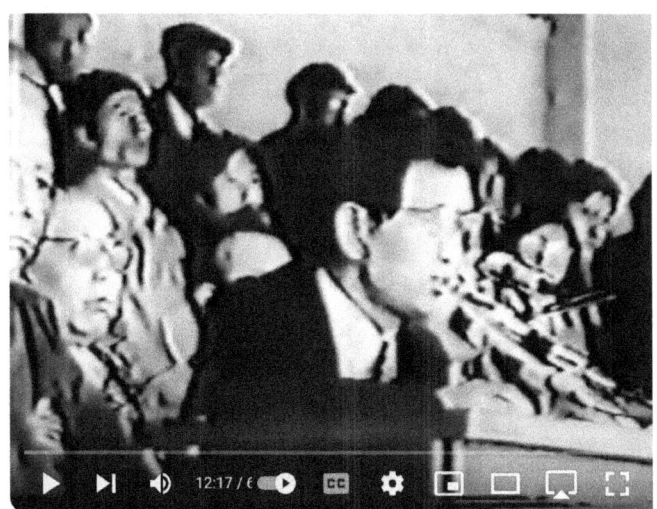

严新1994 5 17沈阳六万人带功报告六小时完整 标清 标清

Dr. Yan Xin Lecturing Tens of Thousands with External Qi, in Shenyang, in 1994

Approximately forty books have been authored about him, and his remarkable work has been extensively documented on numerous videotapes. It's worth noting that Dr. Yan Xin did not personally accept monetary compensation for his work or presentations; instead, the proceeds from these activities were directed toward charitable organizations or scientific research.

严新1987中央党校带功学术报告4小时半 标清

Dr. Yan Xin's Qi Gong Lecture at the Party School of the CCP Central Committee in 1987

In recognition of his exceptional contributions to American society, Dr Yan Xin received several notable honors and acknowledgements. The State Government of California bestowed upon him the status of an honorary citizen. Furthermore, a college in Hawaii granted him an honorary M.D. degree. His work also garnered the attention of President George Bush, who invited him to visit the White House twice and commended him as *"the contemporary sage."*

Dr. Yan Xin with President George Bush

The most important contribution made by Dr. Yan Xin is his groundbreaking study of Qi Gong, an old Chinese cultural legacy, using cutting-edge scientific methods and techniques. His work frequently produces results that are unexpected and thought-provoking. His work has the potential to usher in a new era of contemporary science and improve the progress of mankind. Although some of the claims about the benefits of Qi Gong may seem improbable, Dr. Yan Xin has worked hard to objectively document and validate them. This emphasizes how important it is for modern science to keep an open mind while dealing with new challenges.

Furthermore, Dr. Yan Xin's research has contributed to removing the centuries-long shroud of secrecy that surrounds Chinese Qi Gong and opening it up to a wider audience. Chinese masters of Qi Gong have acknowledged that this profound practice belongs to all mankind, not only the Chinese people, emphasizing the relevance of Qi Gong's worldwide application.

Dr. Yan Xin's impact went well beyond his professional activities. His influence extended beyond his own projects. He not only frequently delivered talks at major universities like Harvard and Qing Hua university and in stadiums to crowds that occasionally exceeded 30,000. His Qi Gong lectures reached audiences all over the world, travelling to both China and the United States. A tribute to the enormous reservoir of knowledge he has freely shared with the world is the large number of books written by various editors and organizations dedicated to his work.

Dr. Yan Xin was unique in his ability to overcome challenges that seemed insurmountable. He provided remedies in situations where others had struggled or failed, reviving faith in the healing profession. His life story demonstrated the amazing confluence of old wisdom and current medical advancements, serving as a tribute to the limitless potential inherent in human existence.

Dr. Yan Xin giving a 5-hour qigong lecture at Harvard University Science Center on July 27, 1996 with an audience of over 1,000 which overflowed into an adjacent lecture hall after only two days' advance notice.

严新医生以贵宾身份
与加拿大总理让·克雷蒂
安会见（此片由本人签字
赠送）

Dr. Yan Xin, with Some World Leaders

Yan Xin Qi Gong

The journey of Dr. Yan Xin goes beyond being successful; it is a tribute to the enduring virtues of fortitude and knowledge. His legacy embodies the mark of a contemporary sage whose influence transcends boundaries and has a significant and long-lasting influence on humanity.

According to Yan Xin Qigong's website[36], "During the past decades, a considerable number of accomplished scientists from leading universities and research institutes in China and the US, such as Tsinghua University, the University of California (UCSD, UCLA) and Harvard University, have applied modern scientific methods and protocols to investigate biological, chemical, and physical effects of Yan Xin Qigong in critical areas of life science, physical sciences, and technology. The Chinese National Natural Science Foundation has supported some of Yan Xin Qigong's research projects.

A large body of scientific data on Yan Xin Qigong's phenomena and effects has been

---

[36] https://yanxinqigong.net/research/index.html

scientifically documented. They have been reviewed by the then Chairman of the Chinese Association of Science and Technology, Dr. Qian Xuesen (Tsien Hsue-Shen), to be "new scientific discoveries and the prelude to scientific revolution". Prof. Hans-Peter Duerr, colleague and successor of Werner Heisenberg as Director of the Institute of Theoretical Physics in Germany, proclaimed the Yan Xin Qigong research results to be "within my window of acceptance."

The external Qi of Yan Xin Qigong has been scientifically detected, and its effects on matters and organisms have been rigorously measured. These research data have established that the external qi of Yan Xin Qigong:

- physically exists.
- can interact with and affect matter from molecular to atomic levels.
- can affect the fundamental components of living organisms (water, sugar, cell membrane, proteins, DNA and RNA).
- can recognize and optimize genetic properties without adverse effects.

- can be applied in biotechnology, materials processing, and chemical reactions."

I became engrossed in a thrilling chapter that played out throughout the exciting last two decades of the 20th century as I dug further into the fascinating life of Dr. Yan Xin. A scientific revolution that effortlessly connected the East and the West during this period of remarkable change. Dr. Yan Xin, a man shrouded in mystery and endowed with great wisdom, stood at the centre of this movement.

I envisioned, a cross-cultural collaboration that had brought together outstanding brains from prestigious institutions like Brigham & Women's Hospital[37] at Harvard University, the Chinese Academy of Sciences, and Tsinghua University... To explore the undiscovered territories of Traditional Chinese Qi Gong, these people came together with a shared curiosity and an unwavering passion.

My mind toured a laboratory where the ordinary transcends into the extraordinary. The unseen

---

[37] https://www.hsph.harvard.edu/profile/delia-wolf-christiani/

became visible, the intangible acquired form and the realms of science and spirituality converged seamlessly within this carefully controlled environment. The fundamental building blocks of life, proteins, and enzymes, appeared to respond to the subtle yet potent influence of Dr. Yan's external Qi as if they were dancing to a new rhythm, revealing the profound connection between Qi Gong and our very existence.

The enchantment didn't cease with proteins and enzymes; now, consider DNA, the intricate biological code of life, reacting to the influence of Dr. Yan's external Qi. This revelation shattered the confines of what we had previously believed possible.

Dr. Yan Xin's collaborations with some of the world's foremost scientists transcended not just mere scientific research; they symbolized the convergence of two distinct worlds. The barriers that once separated them dissolved as the East met the West, as contemporary science intertwined with ancient traditions. Dr. Yan Xin was not merely conducting experiments; he was in the process of redefining the essence of human existence.

Dr. Yan Xin emerged as a prominent figure during these investigations, a trailblazer who fearlessly challenged the established boundaries of our understanding of the human body and its astounding capabilities. His work was nothing short of revolutionary, serving as an open invitation to explore the uncharted territories where the realms of science and spirituality intersected.

As I delved deeper into the world of Yan Xin Qigong, I came to the profound realization that I had not only entered a realm of tradition but had also stepped into a world of the scientific revolution. In this dynamic environment, the boundaries of knowledge were constantly being pushed, discoveries were unfolding, and paradigms were continuously shifting. By this time, I uncovered more about the potential within myself. However, this newfound knowledge only scratches the surface compared to what I would later discover. This leads me to question why the educational institutions I attended never provided any hints or insights into these revelations.

I had never heard of scientific experiments of this nature prior to 2023, although I surfed YouTube science documentaries daily. Since my father passed away, a flood of information about life science discoveries has poured into my life, showing me the direction toward a profound truth that I never believed possible. Is the universe telling me where my father is because it knows I miss him so much?

***

In the realm of exceptional abilities, there exists a fascinating facet of human behavior. On occasion, when we encounter something that challenges our understanding, our natural inclination is to dismiss it. This exact situation unfolded when I endeavored to showcase something remarkable yet undeniably genuine to my husband, Ken, and his father, Gerry. Both have impressive educational backgrounds. Ken is a thriving lawyer, while Gerry is a celebrated medical doctor.

I shared videos showcasing Qi Gong masters performing what appeared to be impossible feats, presented articles authored by esteemed scientists, and provided testimonies from credible witnesses who themselves were scientists... Despite the credibility of the sources, Ken and Gerry just simply believe they couldn't be true.

Official Document Signed By Dr. Qian Xuesen

Cellular Physiology and Biochemistry

Cell Physiol Biochem 2018;49:911-919

Accepted: 27 August 2018

Original Paper

YXQ-EQ Induces Apoptosis and Inhibits Signaling Pathways Important for Metastasis in Non-Small Cell Lung Carcinoma Cells

Xin Yan[a,b] Hua Shen[b] Hongjian Jiang[c] Dan Hu[d] Jun Wang[b] Xinqi Wu[e]

[a]Chongqing Institute of Traditional Chinese Medicine, Chongqing, China, [b]New Medical Science Research Institute, New York, [c]Cardiovascular Clinical Science Foundation, Boston, [d]Brigham and Women's Hospital and Harvard Medical School, Boston, [e]Dana-Farber Cancer Institute and Harvard Medical School, Boston, USA

Cellular Physiology and Biochemistry

Volume 31, Issue 1
February 2013

RESEARCH ARTICLES | JANUARY 25 2013

External Qi of Yan Xin Qigong Inhibits Activation of Akt, Erk1/2 and NF-κB and Induces Cell Cycle Arrest and Apoptosis in Colorectal Cancer Cells

Subject Area: ○ Further Areas

Xin Yan; Hua Shen; Hongjian Jiang; Dan Hu; Jun Wang; Xinqi Wu

Cellular Physiology and Biochemistry (2013) 31 (1): 113–122.
https://doi.org/10.1159/000343354   Article history

ARTICLE CONTENTS

Abstract
Introduction

THE JOURNEY TO AWAKENING 91

SPRINGER LINK

Find a journal   Publish with us   Search

Home > Molecular and Cellular Biochemistry > Article

Published: 10 December 2011

External Qi of Yan Xin Qigong induces cell death and gene expression alterations promoting apoptosis and inhibiting proliferation, migration and glucose metabolism in small-cell lung cancer cells

Xin Yan, Feng Li, Igor Dozmorov, Mark Barton Frank, Ming Dao, Michael Centola, Wei Cao & Dan Hu

Molecular and Cellular Biochemistry 363, 245–255 (2012) | Cite this article

1610 Accesses | 14 Citations | 1216 Altmetric | Metrics

AACR JOURNALS

CANCER PREVENTION RESEARCH

ABOUT   ARTICLES   FOR AUTHORS   ALERTS   NEWS   CANCER HALLMARKS   WEBINARS

Volume 3, Issue 1_Supplement
January 2010

POSTER PRESENTATIONS - PROFFERED ABSTRACTS | OCTOBER 21 2014

Abstract B47: External Qi of Yan Xin Qigong induces cell cycle arrest and apoptosis in colon cancer cells through regulation of multiple signaling pathways FREE

Xin Yan; Hua Shen; Hongjian Jiang; Dan Hu; Chengsheng Zhang; Jun Wang; Xinqi Wu

Check for updates

+ Author & Article Information

Cancer Prev Res (Phila) (2010) 3 (1_Supplement): B47.

https://doi.org/10.1158/1940-6207.PREV-09-B47

Prof. Hans-Peter Duerr, past director of Werner Heisenberg Institute of Theoretical Physics, successor to Werner Heisenberg and Albert Einstein, delivering a keynote speech at the New Century First National Conference on Bigu Manifestation, Health Effects and Scientific Research of Yan Xin Qigong at the Pennsylvania State University, June 23-25, 2000. Prof. Duerr proclaimed that "I am fascinated by these (Yan Xin Qigong) research results...They are within my window of acceptance."

They struggled to believe that these miracles really happened and could happen to anyone who seriously practices Qi Gong.

Consequently, I assumed the role of an investigator, proactively scouring for supplementary information that could elucidate the intricacies of existence beyond our conventional understanding. In the expansive chasm that separates our current knowledge from the enigmas awaiting discovery, I endeavored to build a connection. In this pursuit, the web of stars blinked at me again and showed a path toward my spiritual awakening.

THE JOURNEY TO AWAKENING

✱✱ *Star 5* ✱✱

I came across a 2012's lecture by Professor Lee Si Chen, the former president of the National University of Taiwan, at the Taipei Municipal Library. Professor Lee holds both a master's and a doctoral degree in electrical engineering from Stanford University.

During this lecture, Professor Lee delved into the topic of "The Science of Body, Mind & Soul –

Examining the Authenticity of Exceptional Abilities of the Human Body."[38]

By that point, I had a firm belief in the validity of these miracle phenomena, yet I struggled to persuade my husband, Ken, and his father, Gerry, to share my perspective. Therefore, I was excited when I discovered a reputable scientist who could provide a scientific explanation supported by rigorous academic experiments. In fact, his lecture not only expanded my worldview but also gave me the Universe. Literally, *the Universe.*

In the lecture, Professor Lee shared insights from his 17 years of scientific research focused on Qi Gong and the potential Exceptional Abilities of children. He highlighted China's significant advancements in this field since 1979, with a special emphasis on the extraordinary scientific contributions of Dr. Yan Xin. Professor Lee specifically chose to work with young children in his research, because young children are more likely to develop various Exceptional Abilities after a brief training compared to adults. He has trained numerous young children in

---

[38] https://youtu.be/b1Kdtdo_qqE?si=5FL_dBfpJvhsNTDS

both Taiwan and the United States to unlock their exceptional potential.

During his presentation, Professor Lee provided an illustrative example from one of his training sessions at Stanford University. Each training session lasted for only four days, with two hours of training per day. In this session, there were 173 trainees, and remarkably, by the end of the four days, 41 children had developed the ability to read using their fingers instead of their eyes.

Notably, one of these children achieved this skill after just three days of training. Professor Lee acknowledged that these numbers might not be statistically significant enough to represent the entire population. However, they did serve as compelling evidence that such Exceptional Abilities exist and are not as rare or impossible as commonly believed.

Professor Lee's Training Session

Professor Lee emphasized that many individuals possess a wide range of Exceptional Abilities naturally. However, these abilities often go unnoticed or unacknowledged because people don't believe in things they can't see. During his extensive 11 years of research, Professor Lee encountered over a thousand individuals who exhibited such Exceptional Abilities. Some had developed these abilities through the practice of Qi Gong, while others possessed them as innate talents.

Among these individuals were notable figures such as a medical doctor, an academician of

Academia Sinica, and a former president of the National University of Taiwan. Additionally, one person held the position of chairman on the board of a major public company in China, and another was a professor at Qing Hua University. The people who possess such Exceptional Abilities were not limited to specific professions or backgrounds; they could be found among lawyers, journalists, students, housewives, workers, and even peasants, indicating that such abilities were widespread and could manifest in individuals from all walks of life.

Professor Lee shared a compelling true story about one of his students who possessed clairvoyant eyesight and could see through objects. When this student first disclosed his exceptional ability to his parents during childhood, they dismissed it as an implausible notion and believed he might be experiencing mental health issues. As time passed, the student's mother eventually came to accept the reality when he reached his teenage years. However, his father remained believing that his son was dealing with a mental problem.

This poignant story provided valuable insight into why individuals like Ken and Gerry refuse to believe the existence of such miraculous phenomena. They must have direct experience to believe it's true, or they must hear from the authorities they trust.

***

During that captivating lecture, Professor Lee delved into the fascinating world of finger reading, with a particular focus on the remarkable journey of a young girl named Maie Takahashi. As he unravelled the details of this groundbreaking research project, I found myself in awe of the extraordinary human potential on full display. Professor Lee's discoveries not only expanded my horizons but also sparked a profound curiosity that compelled me to revisit religious texts because I might have misunderstood or overlooked their deeper meanings before.

In my quest for understanding, I couldn't help but wonder whether the fusion of modern scientific exploration, as exemplified by Professor Lee's lecture and the timeless teachings of religious texts, could lead to a more holistic comprehension of our existence. Indeed, in an age where scientific knowledge seems to have surpassed all bounds, it was intriguing to consider what wisdom and insights might still lie dormant within these ancient scriptures, waiting to be reinterpreted through the lens of our evolving understanding of human potential.

In this newfound journey, I was motivated to explore the convergence of science and spirituality, as both appeared to hold keys to unlocking the boundless capabilities of human experience. It was a reminder that our quest for knowledge knows no bounds and that the most profound revelations might be found where we least expect them.

Professor Lee's remarkable research project spanned 11 years, commencing when Ms. Mair Takahashi was a mere 11 years old. Residing in the vibrant city of Los Angeles, California, Maie, along with her devoted mother, embarked on a life-altering odyssey.

The inception of this extraordinary adventure began with a simple television program about "Exceptional Abilities in Japan," which Maie's mother stumbled upon when her daughter was a tender ten years old. Little did they know that this moment of serendipity would change the course of their lives forever. It was through this fateful encounter with the TV program that Maie's mother first glimpsed the astonishing mental faculties that her daughter possessed.

Motivated and inspired by this revelation, Maie's mother decided to take an incredible leap of faith. She sought out the guidance of Professor Lee and, with unwavering determination, enrolled her daughter in his transformative training sessions. These sessions would prove to be the crucible in which Maie's "Third Eye[39]" was not only tested but also opened, unlocking a world of possibilities that would boggle the mind and challenge conventional understanding.

The saga of Ms. Maie Takahashi, a young prodigy hailing from the bustling city of Los Angeles, served as a powerful testimony to the seemingly limitless potential embedded within each of us. Her journey, catalyzed by her mother's unwavering belief in her exceptional abilities, offered a poignant reminder

---

[39] In Buddhism, the third eye is said to be located around the middle of the forehead, Buddhists regard the third eye as the "eye of consciousness", representing the vantage point from which enlightenment beyond one's physical sight is achieved.

https://en.wikipedia.org/wiki/Third_eye

of the uncharted frontiers of human potential waiting to be explored. With Professor Lee's expert guidance, this narrative took an unprecedented turn, uncovering layers of human cognition that defied conventional understanding.

Ms. Maie Takahashi's participation in these transformative sessions was nothing less than extraordinary. Her exceptional abilities shone brilliantly, capturing the attention and admiration of Professor Lee. Recognizing the remarkable potential within her, he made a pivotal decision to handpick her, along with two other young prodigies, for an exciting collaborative venture in the realm of life science research at National Taiwan University.

This captivating tale serves as a testament to the power of recognizing and nurturing Exceptional Abilities. It underscores the significance of opportunities like Professor Lee's unique training and research programs. Maie's journey exemplifies how, when extraordinary talents are identified and cultivated, they can lead to groundbreaking advancements and contribute significantly to our understanding of the universe and life.

While researching Ms. Maie Takahashi's groundbreaking Finger Reading experiments, I came across an intriguing article that shed light on a critical juncture in her journey. At the tender age of 16, Ms. Takahashi found herself under the scrutiny of a group of skeptical scientists and graduate students who harbored doubts about the legitimacy of Professor Lee's experiment[40]. In response to concerns related to potential fraud or bias, this inquisitive group embarked on a quest to conduct their own investigation.

To address the prevailing doubts, these individuals ingeniously devised a distinct and impartial approach. Each member of this group meticulously inscribed a Chinese character or selected a color without any discernible shape on a plain piece of paper. With methodical care, they collected these nondescript test materials, shrouding them in anonymity, and placed them within a black bag for Ms. Maie Takahashi to touch with her fingers, one piece at a time. This process meticulously generated an unbiased and entirely random set of objects for their experimental endeavors.

---

[40] https://www.sohu.com/a/333147807_120272656

This methodical and impartial procedure not only underscored their dedication to uncovering the truth but also reflected the essence of scientific inquiry, where skepticism and meticulous examination are the cornerstones of advancement. The contents of that unassuming bag would soon become a pivotal element in unravelling the mysteries surrounding Finger Reading and its exceptional practitioners.

The results of this rigorous experimentation and the subsequent impact it had on Ms. Takahashi's journey undoubtedly stand as a riveting and pivotal chapter in the ongoing narrative of extraordinary human potential and the relentless pursuit of scientific truth. This episode not only serves as a testament to the ever-evolving quest for knowledge but also illuminates the resilience of the human spirit when faced with skepticism and the need for rigorous validation.

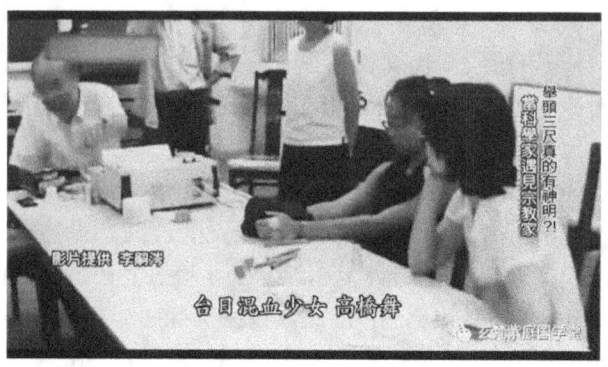

Ms. Takahashi was entrusted with the unique challenge of touching each of these nondescript papers one by one with her finger. In a remarkable display of her exceptional abilities, she astoundingly achieved a flawless identification rate of 100% for each item. This extraordinary outcome not only showcased the remarkable extent of her capabilities but also offered incontrovertible evidence validating the existence of such mind power.

This skeptical group of scientists became even more intrigued when Ms. Takahashi couldn't identify a particular word and instead described seeing the shape of a man with light around him. The word turned out to be "佛," which means Buddha in Chinese. To test if this was an illusion, they wrote the same words in different languages and had Ms. Takahashi attempt to read them. Surprisingly, she could not see any of the written words but consistently described seeing the image of a man with light around him.

The experience with Ms. Takahashi's Finger Reading experiment propelled the group to delve even deeper into the realm of spirituality and exploration. They decided to explore more sacred and revered words, including "Jesus Christ," "Bodhisattva," and "Bhaisajyaguru." However, they encountered a fascinating twist: instead of merely perceiving words on her Third Eye screen, Ms. Takahashi began to witness vivid images bathed in light.

This revelation sparked a novel hypothesis among the inquisitive group. They postulated that these sacred keywords might function as the equivalent of website addresses, serving as gateways to the inner "homepages" of the respective holy spirits. In this intriguing line of inquiry, they suggested Ms. Takahashi to try the "homepage" of Bhaisajyaguru.

To accomplish this, she was encouraged to meditate and think in her mind, "May I come in to visit?" [41]

This remarkable exploration not only expanded the boundaries of human understanding but also exemplified the symbiotic relationship between scientific inquiry and spirituality. It was a journey where the mystical met the analytical and where Ms. Takahashi's unique gift offered access into uncharted territory.

Ms. Takahashi heeded the advice, and, in an extraordinary moment, her Third Eye screen revealed a stunning revelation. A luminous, imposing figure appeared on her Third Eye screen, radiating an aura of brilliance. This ethereal being then posed a question, "Which one would you like to visit?"

Ms. Takahashi, with grace and conviction, responded, "the Number 8." The resplendent figure acknowledged her choice, and in an instant, her Third Eye screen showed her to a breathtaking realm. Before she unfurled a magnificent botanic garden

---

[41] https://sclee.website/wp-content/uploads/2020/04/traveling-around-the-visible-and-invisible-wordls.pdf

adorned with spherical, luminescent flowers that bathed the entire landscape in their radiant glow. The scene was nothing short of a visual masterpiece.

As her experience continued to unfold, the Third Eye screen gradually receded, leaving Ms. Takahashi and her audience awestruck by the transcendental journey she had embarked upon. This extraordinary encounter opened a new world of wonder and curiosity, fusing the spiritual and the scientific worlds in a unique and spellbinding tapestry of exploration.

With a thirst for further exploration, Ms. Takahashi once more ventured into the mystical realm of her Third Eye screen. She inquired in her mind, "May I see another one, the Number 6?"

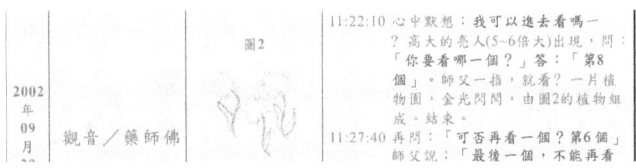

Screenshot of Professor Lee's Experiment Report

The screen responded to her request, and the radiant figure informed her that this would be the final revelation, with no more to follow. Soon, the screen materialized, unveiling yet another breathtaking botanic garden. This time, it was a mesmerizing vine series characterized by its soft, ethereal nature and delicate transparency. The leaves of the vines possessed a unique luminescence, with their edges emitting a radiant light.

As Ms. Takahashi absorbed the beauty and wonder of this final garden, the screen slowly dissolved, concluding her remarkable journey in the mystical world. The blend of science and spirituality produced a tapestry of awe-inspiring experiences that would forever leave an indelible mark on the hearts of all who witnessed this astonishing exploration.

09月29日	觀音／藥師佛	圖3	11:27:40 再問：「可否再看一個？第6個」師父說：「最後一個，不能再看了」，一指就看？另一片植物園，蔓藤由上垂下，軟的，半透明，飄來飄去，尖端發光，看了感覺非常好。 11:36:13「可否不撰字條，就逕去看那些美好的景象？」，師父回答：「可以但我不一定在」 11:38:15「可否告訴我第6及第8個樂園的名稱？」，師父答「說了，你們也不知道，不說」

Screenshot of Professor Lee's Experiment Report

Ms. Takahashi asked in her mind, "may I go in to look at those beautiful scenes without touching the paper?"

The shining man replied, "Yes, you may, but I might not be here."

Ms. Takahashi asked in her mind again, "Could you please tell me the names of the medicine gardens, numbers 6 and 8?

The shining man responded, "You can't know even if I told you no."

According to Professor Lee, this enigmatic shining man who had appeared on Ms. Takahashi's Third Eye screen was a towering presence, standing at a remarkable height – roughly 5-6 times that of an ordinary man. Although Ms. Takahashi couldn't discern his facial features due to the radiant brilliance emanating from his head, the team surmised that this awe-inspiring figure might indeed be Bhaisaijyaguru. It was a profound encounter that left them contemplating the possibility that even spiritual entities ventured out from their spiritual abode to engage in other activities rather than remaining eternally on their "websites."

***

However, a practical challenge emerged. The schedule for their experiments often overlapped with Ms. Takahashi's spiritual practices. Occasionally, her spiritual guide's presence would inadvertently disrupt their experiments. To address this issue and gain a deeper understanding, Professor Lee's team resolved to conduct an interview with Ms. Takahashi's spiritual guide using the Finger Reading method.

In preparation for this unique interview, they assembled ten pieces of paper, each inscribed with 1-2 questions. This innovative approach demonstrated their commitment to exploring the intersection of science and spirituality while seeking to harmonize the two in Ms. Takahashi's remarkable journey.

Ms. Takahashi found this new experiment to be especially captivating and beneficial for a unique reason. It provided a refreshing departure from her usual method of reading papers with her Third Eye, which demanded an intense focus of her mind. In this experimental setup, she simply placed her fingers on the paper contained within a dark bag and meditated.

As she made this tactile connection, her Third Eye screen illuminated and then gradually faded away.

However, the true marvel lay in the subsequent phases of this experiment. When her Third Eye screen rekindled its radiance, she could either hear the answers from her spiritual guide or see him directly on the screen. This method introduced a streamlined process, significantly enhancing her ability to receive guidance and information.

Ordinarily, it took her three cycles of her Third Eye screen lighting up to read just one word. This innovative approach offered a more efficient and direct channel of communication with her spiritual guide, enriching her experiences and deepening her understanding of the spiritual realm.

The interview questions and responses provide intriguing insights into Ms. Takahashi's communication with her spiritual guide:

Questions regarding the Universe:

1) Question: Teacher, please tell us, how do you think the universe came into existence?

Answer: Big Bang, later God helped.

2) Question: Teacher, please tell us your view on this, aside from our physical universe, do other physical universes exist?
Answer: Yes, but they are very distant.

Questions regarding the Origin of Life:

1) Question: Teacher, please tell us your view on how did primitive life forms in the universe come into existence? Was it through random evolution or created by God?
Answer: Mostly through random evolution.

2) Question: Teacher, how did human beings on earth come into existence?

Answer: Silent.

3) Question: Teacher, how did human beings on earth come into existence? Why didn't you answer the question the last time?
Answer: Laugh out loud... it was too difficult to answer.

These responses provide a glimpse into the enigmatic and sometimes elusive nature of the communication between Ms. Takahashi and her spiritual guide. The questions touch upon profound topics, from the origin of the universe to the emergence of life on Earth, offering unique perspectives on matters that have captivated human curiosity for centuries.

These questions and responses continue to provide a thought-provoking glimpse into the intriguing dialogue between Ms. Takahashi and her spiritual guide.

Questions regarding Spirits:

1) Question: Teacher, please tell us, how did the spirits come into existence?
   Answer: Hm...most likely through evolution from earlier spirits.

2) Question: Teacher, please tell us, does time exist in your world?
   Answer: There is no limit for me.

Questions regarding Aliens:

1) Question: Teacher, please tell us, when will human beings on Earth contact alien civilizations?
   Answer: Not already there?

2) Question: Teacher, please tell us, are you in the spiritual world or on another planet?
   A: Anywhere.

3) Question: Teacher, are you an alien?
   A: Half, half.

These exchanges open doors to further contemplation about the nature of existence, the fluidity of time, the possibilities of extraterrestrial contact, and the enigmatic qualities of Ms. Takahashi's spiritual guide, leaving room for endless exploration and curiosity.

The experiment conducted on January 13th, 2002, brought the research team a remarkable revelation. During this session, they uncovered an extraordinary facet of Ms. Takahashi's [42] spiritual guide: the ability to hear and see the team directly, bypassing the need to communicate through Ms. Takahashi.

To maintain the utmost secrecy and prevent any potential information leakage, the team had placed notes with questions in Ms. Takahashi's hand, concealed within a bag. This ensured that none of the team members were privy to the specific questions contained in the notes. That means, during the experiment, none of the participants knew what question was asked nor the answer for what question. They would only know after everything was done and matching the answers at another meeting.

However, during a discussion about the renowned figure Nostradamus, Ms. Takahashi's spiritual guide unexpectedly communicated with her in Chinese (and occasionally in English), stating, "This is the question in your discussion; please continue your discussion!" This revelation highlighted the spiritual guide's remarkable ability to not only

---

[42] https://sclee.website/wp-content/uploads/2020/04/information-field-5_5.pdf

perceive the team's conversation but also actively engage in their discourse.

日 期	正確答案	透視結果	實驗過程記錄
2002年1月13日	請師父開示 為何上次手掌透字 不清楚，有一個了開示 把 Nozira Lm的看式 的精℃來		16:14:40 起 16:19:04 □去了 16:23:58 （看到師父）一直在笑 16:24:12 "這個問題就是你們在討論的，你們就繼續討論吧！" （的確正在討論此事）
2002年1月13日	我心情了無開示 況從 那裡來 今生 使命其的 正道修屬來		17:04:30 起 17:10:32 "這個講了就無趣" 17:11:55 沒了

圖　八

Screenshot of Lab Experiment Report

Upon recognizing that Ms. Takahashi's spiritual guide could indeed hear them directly and even discern their thoughts, the research team sought confirmation of this extraordinary capability. Their inquiry led to a revelation: the spiritual guide affirmed that he not only could hear them directly but also possessed knowledge of their thoughts.

Since the team was curious about the alien civilizations, they frequently begged Ms. Takahashi's spiritual guide to take her to visit one of them. Six months later, he agreed to show her one of them on Cygnus, Milky Way, a planet 434 light years away from us, on Ms. Takahashi's Third Eye[43].

Ms. Takahashi's account of her visit to the alien civilization in Cygnus[44], Milky Way, was nothing short of extraordinary. She relayed her observations to Professor Lee, describing the inhabitants of this distant world. According to her reports, the aliens on Cygnus exhibited humanoid characteristics with a single head, two eyes, two nose holes, and a singular mouth. They possessed a pair of hands and a pair of

---

[43] https://youtu.be/a4qPB-jOvuOo?si=wFjRb3DuXcd0mAEq
[44] https://sclee.website/wp-content/uploads/2020/04/traveling-around-the-visible-and-invisible-wordls.pdf

legs, but what set them apart from humans was their distinctive hand structure – each hand had three fingers, with one of these digits notably larger than the others. Additionally, these beings sported two antenna-like appendages on their heads.

The description of these alien life forms painted a fascinating picture of the diversity of life that might exist beyond our planet. This revelation added a new layer of intrigue to the quest for extraterrestrial understanding and underscored the boundless possibilities that may exist in the cosmos. Ms. Takahashi's journey opened a window to the imagination, igniting the curiosity of those who yearned to explore the unknown and uncover the mysteries of the universe.

The vivid details provided by Ms. Takahashi shed further light on the enigmatic civilization she encountered on the distant planet in Cygnus. These alien beings were characterized by their sleek, dark, and lustrous skin that resembled a form-fitting garment. They talk fast.

A particularly fascinating aspect of this civilization was its technology, exemplified by a remarkable machine with an input board. Ms. Takahashi saw that by entering a specific code, something came out from the machine, and then the code inputter put it directly into his mouth. According to Ms. Takahashi's spiritual guide, this civilization's technological prowess far surpassed that of humanity.

To validate the authenticity of Ms. Takahashi's extraordinary observations, Professor Lee decided to enlist the expertise of Ms. Sun Chu Lin, an individual renowned for her elevated psychic abilities. Despite Ms. Takahshi and Ms. Sun having no prior knowledge of each other and no communication between them, they both reported the same about what they saw on that particular planet in Cygnus.

They both attested to the presence of antenna-like structures on the heads of these extraterrestrial beings. The synchronicity of their accounts not only provided compelling evidence that what they witnessed was not a product of their individual illusions, but they also added a layer of credibility to the existence of the alien civilization on that remote planet in Cygnus. This unanticipated alignment in their experiences was a testament to the authenticity of their observations and further deepened the mystery and wonder of their exploration.

The revelation that these alien beings possessed not just one but two antennas on their heads, one for sending and one for receiving, added a fascinating layer of complexity to their understanding of this extraterrestrial civilization. Since Ms. Takahashi had initially reported the presence of two antennas, but Ms. Sun only saw one. So, she took the opportunity to inquire with one of the alien beings about the presence of a single antenna by asking in her mind. The alien responded by showing his other antenna.

This enlightening exchange underscored the significance of open and direct communication. It not only resolved the apparent discrepancy in Ms. Takahashi and Ms. Sun's observations but also deepened our understanding of this alien civilization's capacity for direct communication from consciousness to consciousness without having to share a common language. This discovery reminded me of the Tower of Babel[45] from *The Bible*. Could it be true that the

---

[45] https://en.wikipedia.org/wiki/Tower_of_Babel#Confusion_of_tongues

tower symbolized human greed for material possessions and consumptions and that greed caused us to lose our innate gifts? Could it be true that we didn't need any language at all at the beginning of life on Earth?

The discovery of the antenna-like feature on the alien beings from Cygnus prompted Professor Lee to consider the intriguing possibility that the ancestors of these aliens might have visited Earth in the past. This hypothesis was fueled by an intriguing artifact: a 5,800-year-old ancient stela that was exhibited at the Museum of Hu Bei in 2014. The stela depicted an image of a person adorned with an antenna-like feature on the head, which did not align with any known aspects of recorded Chinese culture.

Intrigued by this ancient artifact and its potential connection to the alien beings from Cygnus, Professor Lee sought validation. He reached out to Ms. Takahashi's spiritual guide, who had offered invaluable insights into their previous experiments, to inquire about this assumption. To Professor Lee's amazement, the invisible spiritual guide agreed with his assumption.

Professor Lee's discovery that aliens could directly communicate with human beings from Earth through consciousness helped me to understand something that I thought was impossible.

Ten years ago, a friend who had liver cancer started to practice Buddhism. He was fascinated with both Buddhism and alien-related news, and he liked to forward me such articles on social media. I took his kindness for granted and refused to believe in anything he sent to me.

How could any human being communicate with an alien since they don't share the same language? For this one reason, I rejected all his efforts to help me learn more. Now that friend is gone, and

I started to really understand what *The Heart Sutra*[46] revealed[47].

---

[46] https://en.wikipedia.org/wiki/Heart_Sutra

[47] The Heart Sutra in English:

Om Homage to the Perfection of Wisdom the Lovely, the Holy!

Avalokita, the Holy Lord and Bodhisattva, was moving in the deep course of the Wisdom which has gone beyond.

He looked down from on high, He beheld but five heaps, and He saw that in their own-being they were empty.

Here, O Sariputra,

form is emptiness and the very emptiness is form;

emptiness does not differ from form, form does not differ from emptiness, whatever is emptiness, that is form,

the same is true of feelings, perceptions, impulses, and consciousness.

Here, O Sariputra,

all dharmas are marked with emptiness;

they are not produced or stopped, not defiled or immaculate, not deficient or complete.

Therefore, O Sariputra,

in emptiness there is no form nor feeling, nor perception, nor impulse, nor consciousness;

No eye, ear, nose, tongue, body, mind; No forms, sounds, smells, tastes, touchables or objects of mind; No sight-organ element, and so forth, until we come to:

No mind-consciousness element; There is no ignorance, no extinction of ignorance, and so forth, until we come to: There is no decay and death, no extinction of decay and death. There is no suffering, no origination, no stopping, no path.

There is no cognition, no attainment and no non-attainment.

Therefore, O Sariputra,

it is because of his non-attainmentness that a Bodhisattva, through having relied on the Perfection of Wisdom, dwells without thought-coverings. In the absence of thought-coverings he has not been made to tremble,

he has overcome what can upset, and in the end he attains to Nirvana.

All those who appear as Buddhas in the three periods of time fully awake to the utmost, right and perfect Enlightenment because they have relied on the Perfection of Wisdom.

Therefore, one should know the prajnaparamita as the great spell, the spell of great knowledge, the utmost spell, the unequalled spell, allayer of all suffering, in truth -- for

THE JOURNEY TO AWAKENING

It's remarkable how profound discoveries and insights can shed new light on age-old wisdom and beliefs. I finally realized that this concise sutra was telling the ultimate truth of the universe and life in terms of consciousness and matter.

The wisdom of *The Heart Sutra* has given me the power to maintain a peaceful mind while going through those challenging times. However, my understanding remained superficial for another ten

---

what could go wrong? By the prajnaparamita has this spell been delivered. It runs like this:

gate gate paragate parasamgate bodhi svaha.

(Gone, gone, gone beyond, gone altogether beyond, O what an awakening, all-hail! --)

This completes the Heart of perfect Wisdom.

years. I knew that the Buddha Shakamuni was a fully enlightened man with superior wisdom, but I didn't know that his other name Tathagata[48] means – from the *Ultimate Truth*. I thought no human being could know the ultimate truth of the Universe, no matter how wise one is. Of course, I couldn't understand why emptiness and existence could coexist. Now, I know that I had missed 99+% of the wisdom conveyed by this unsurpassed, profound, subtle, wonderful sutra.

Professor Lee's remarkable findings connected the dots that I thought were unrelated before, especially his application of the Quantum Wave Function[49]. In Chinese tradition, we call the visible world Yang Space, and then we call the invisible world, where angels and ghosts live, Yin Space. In

---

[48] The Buddha's other name Tathagata in Chinese is 如来, means from the ultimate truth.
https://en.wikipedia.org/wiki/Tathāgata

[49] A Quantum Wave Function is a complex-valued mathematical description of a quantum state of a particle as a function of momentum, time, position, and spin.

https://en.wikipedia.org/wiki/Wave_function

an interview[50], Professor Lee applied the concept of the complex number[51] in the Quantum Wave Function to explain the invisible nature of the Yin Space.

So, the real number component represents an existence manifested in the Yang Space that we can see, and the imaginary component represents the same existence in the Yin Space[52] that we can't see. Since every physical existence is formed by quantum particles, it has a visible and an invisible component. However, as Professor Lee pointed out, not every

---

[50] https://youtu.be/IB0G1iS5uuk?si=YtHw-ojxD_zHZlNp

[51] A complex number looks like this: 1+2i. 1 is a real number that we can find it from a one-dimensional axis. 2i is an imagined number that we must find it from another dimension.

https://en.wikipedia.org/wiki/Complex_number

[52] I later learned that the Yin Space and Yang Space are in the same space. We just need to have different brainwave frequencies to connect/detect various existences. Just like how we can't see the electric fan blades when they spin fast, then visible when the fan slows down.

existence in the Universe is manifested in the Yang Space, and the Yang Space is within the Yin Space.

Wikipedia summarized it nicely: when a particle is measured, there is a 100% probability that it must be somewhere. When someone was answering Professor Lee's questionnaire, although he was invisible, he must exist somewhere. My stubborn, materialistic belief shook more and more vibrantly.

In fact, the concept of an invisible spiritual guide isn't new for those who have their Third Eye opened or the Qi Gong/Yoga practitioners. Without learning the details about Professor Lee's research[53], I would never have believed in their existence. I always believed that's something from people's imagination or autosuggestion from any picked-up signs. When Ms. Sun Chu Lin talked about her several spiritual guides, she mentioned a few aliens and

---

[53] Details of Professor Lee's research with spirits recounted in this video:

https://youtu.be/sm2zar9v-so?si=twnYCLErJHdicbYf

historical figures like Lao Tzu[54] and Kong Ming[55]. I thought she credited her own wisdom and hard work to the ancient sages she admired. I couldn't believe that they had indeed directly educated her in person.

---

[54] https://plato.stanford.edu/entries/laozi/

[55] https://youtu.be/1-snzy91VEI?si=Ac-MwNWxMxxSFJsiQ

The Buddha's Teachings[56]

Professor Lee's application of the Quantum Wave Function sparked a profound revelation within me. It led me to delve into the profound connection

---

[56]

The Four Noble Truths comprise the essence of Buddha's teachings, though they leave much left unexplained. They are the truth of suffering, the truth of the cause of suffering, the truth of the end of suffering, and the truth of the path that leads to the end of suffering.

https://www.pbs.org/edens/thailand/buddhism.htm#:~:text=The%20Four%20Noble%20Truths%20comprise,to%20the%20end%20of%20suffering.

between the Buddha[57]'s cosmic perspective and the depths of meditation intertwined with the fabric of spacetime. Over the course of my 56 years, I've traversed the globe, visiting countless Buddhist temples, yet the significance of a solitary monk in deep meditation eluded me. Now, it all crystallizes into a beautiful, coherent understanding.

At the heart of this revelation lies a pivotal concept: *Frequency*. It is the key that unlocks these seemingly disparate realms. The resonance of existence, echoing through the vibrations of our thoughts and actions, harmonizes with the very essence of the Universe. Different frequencies are intangible threads woven through the tapestry of reality, binding us to the cosmos in ways I had never fathomed before. I finally understood why there is no secret of the Universe to the Buddhas, all the answers are in the synchronicities, [58] because their frequency

---

[57] https://en.thaythichtructhaiminh.com/early-life-of-prince-siddhartha-gautama-life-of-budda-part-1-d170.html

[58] The **simultaneous** occurrence of events which appear significantly related but have no **discernible causal** connection.

bandwidth is infinity – infinite keys to passthrough infinite dimensions[59].

In this newfound clarity, I see how the serene contemplation of a monk mirrors the cosmic dance of particles and waves. Through meditation, we attune ourselves to the frequencies that underlie the Universe's grand symphony. It is a practice that transcends time and space, allowing us to resonate with the fundamental truths that govern our existence.

As I reflect on this revelation, I find a profound sense of unity between the wisdom of ancient teachings and the cutting-edge insights of quantum physics. It is a testament to the timeless wisdom that emanates from both spiritual introspection and scientific inquiry. This revelation has not only enriched my understanding of the Universe and life but has also deepened my appreciation for the boundless

---

https://en.wikipedia.org/wiki/Synchronicity

[59] Later, I realized that at the infinite dimensions, every point of the space can be the origin. That means, each of us can be the center of the Universe. We do not need to go out to search for the center of the Universe.

wisdom that transcends cultural and temporal boundaries.

In an insightful article published in the National Library of Medicine, titled "Buddha's Brain: Neuroplasticity and Meditation," Harvard-trained neuroscientist Richard J. Davidson and his dedicated team made a groundbreaking discovery. Their research revealed that long-term expert meditators possessed the remarkable ability to generate gamma brain waves, which were 30 times as strong as the new meditator students. Normally, for most individuals, gamma wave bursts last a fraction of a second, but for the monks in this study, the bursts surprisingly lasted for up to a full minute of meditation[60].

---

[60] https://www.diygenius.com/measuring-the-brain-waves-of-buddhist-monks-meditating/#:~:text=For%20most%20people%2C%20gamma%20wave,a%20full%20minute%20of%20meditation.

> **WIRED** Buddha on the Brain
>
> The researchers had never seen anything like it. Worried that something might be wrong with their equipment or methods, they brought in more monks, as well as a control group of college students inexperienced in meditation. The monks produced gamma waves that were 30 times as strong as the students'. In addition, larger areas of the meditators' brains were active, particularly in the left prefrontal cortex, the part of the brain responsible for positive emotions.

Why does gamma brain wave[61] have anything to do with the Buddha's outlook on the Universe and life? Because it enables people to have Out of Body Experience[62]. According to Borijijin and her team, "The temporoparietal junction, a brain region where the temporal and parietal lobes meet, toward the back of the brain behind the ear, was particularly active with gamma waves. This region is known to

---

[61] https://en.wikipedia.org/wiki/Gamma_wave

[62] https://pub-med.ncbi.nlm.nih.gov/16186034/#:~:text=Out%2Of%2Dbody%20experiences%20(,location%20outside%20his%20physical%20body.

be activated when people have out-of-body experiences or dreams."[63]

The significance of this connection between the Buddha's teachings and the gamma brain wave becomes apparent. Especially considering that the longer one can maintain a gamma wave frequency, the more profound their potential for spiritual exploration and transcending the confines of the physical body is.

According to dharmazen.org, truly enlightened, very kind and compassionate practitioners can even achieve *lambda(>100Hz)* and *epsilon (<0.5Hz)* brain waves at the same time[64]. These two waves could coexist because the high-frequency lambda wave is embedded in the low-frequency epsilon

---

[63] https://www.livescience.com/health/neuroscience/surges-of-activity-in-the-dying-human-brain-could-hint-at-fleeting-conscious-experiences#:~:text=The%20temporoparietal%20junction%2C%20a%20brain,experiences%20or%20dreams%2C%20Borjigin%20said.

[64] https://www.dharmazen.org/X2GB/D22Method/M129.htm

wave[65]. "The lambda wave is essentially riding on the epsilon wave." "Lambda is associated with a much higher level of consciousness, beyond simply deep meditation or spiritual consciousness. It is more a state of complete oneness and wholeness."

This makes perfect sense as to why *The Heart Sutra* says that there was no obstacle in space when Avalokitesvara was in Samadhi. As we learned from radio waves, low-frequency radio waves are good for long-distance communications, while high-frequency radio waves are good for short-distance communications. The epsilon waves can bypass obstacles, while the lambda waves can send information almost instantly.

The ability to transcend the limitations of the physical body can lead to a deeper understanding of the Universe and one's place within it. In the Buddhist perspective[66], the cosmos is intricately organized into a hierarchical structure, both in terms of physical space and conscious awareness. This

---

[65] https://www.binauralbeatsfreak.com/brainwave-entrainment/epsilon-waves-lambda-waves

[66] https://en.wikipedia.org/wiki/Buddhist_cosmology

structure provides a profound framework for understanding the Universe.

In terms of spacewise organization, it begins with the concept of a "Small World." Within this framework, one solar system is referred to as a Small World. 1,000[67] of these Small Worlds come together to form a "Small Thousand World" (Galaxy). Further up the scale, 1,000 of these Small Thousand Worlds combine to form a "Middle Thousand World" (Cluster). Finally, at the highest level of spatial organization, 1,000 Middle Thousand Worlds unite to form the grandest scale, termed a "Big Thousand World" (Big Bang).

Then, there are numerous such Big Thousand Worlds in the ten directions of the Dharmahatu[68](Universe). One direction is on the top, one direction is at the bottom, and then eight directions are in between. Each of these Big Thousand Worlds/Big Bangs is referred to as one "Buddha Land" and has

---

[67] Numbers here are not absolute, simply mean numerous.
[68] https://en.wikipedia.org/wiki/Dharma-dhatu#:~:text=Dharmadhātu%20is%20the%20purified%20mind,is%20accessed%20via%20the%20mindstream.

one Buddha responsible for educating all the sentient beings within that land. The Buddha Shakamuni, also known as Guatama Buddha, is specifically responsible for enlightening and guiding all beings within our own Buddha Land, which is commonly referred to as "Saha World[69]."

According to the venerable master Chin Kung[70], in consciouswise, meditators who reach different levels of meditative attainment, specifically the Dhyana Heavens[71], can expand their awareness to experience different scales of the cosmos. This perspective provides a spiritual framework for understanding the interconnectedness of consciousness and the vastness of the Universe:

1. First Dhyana Heaven: Meditators at this level have developed the ability to expand their awareness to the point where it can encompass and experience the entire solar system to acquire worldly

---

[69] https://en.wikipedia.org/wiki/Sahā

[70] https://bookgb.bfnn.org/books/0407.htm

[71] https://en.wikipedia.org/wiki/Dhyana_in_Buddhism

knowledge and a touch of spiritual experience[72].

2. Second Dhyana Heaven: Those who attain the Second Dhyana Heaven can further expand their awareness to cover and experience the entire galaxy.
3. Third Dhyana Heaven: Meditators who reach the Third Dhyana Heaven can extend their awareness to encompass and experience the whole cluster of galaxies.
4. Fourth Dhyana Heaven: For those who achieve the Fourth Dhyana Heaven, meditators can expand their awareness to encompass and experience the entire Big Bang.

However, the goal of dhyana is to go beyond the experience of mind and body to understand the absolute ultimate reality. No words could describe this since it is an experience beyond the mind. So, words can only point at the moon and can't describe the moon.

---

[72] https://www.ncbi.nlm.nih.gov/pmc/articles/PMC3573536/

After practicing meditation for over three decades, Ms. Sun's awareness could reach 434 light years away to see and communicate with those aliens by herself, while Ms. Takahashi had to go through her spiritual guide to experience the same. That makes sense. Professor Lee's Finger Reading study reported [73] that during the experiments, Ms. Takahashi's brain wave frequency stayed at alpha wave (8~13Hz), which is impossible to have an OBE [74] experience that needs gamma wave frequency.

According to the logic of the venerable master of Chin Kung[75], Ms. Sun must have achieved at least the Second Dhyana Heaven. The spirits of the Arhats and the lower-level Bodhisattvas can travel freely within the Big Bang. Still, only the highly accomplished Arhats, Bodhisattvas and Buddhas can travel freely across the Big Bangs. For example, our Big Bang/Saha World is in the south of the Universe,

---

[73] https://sclee.website/wp-content/uploads/2020/04/SCLee-2-2.pdf

[74] https://en.wikipedia.org/wiki/Out-of-body_experience

[75] https://bookgb.bfnn.org/books/0407.htm

but Amitabha Buddha and Avalokitesvara Bodhisattva are from the Western Blissful Pure Land[76]. They are said to be helping all lives throughout the Universe. So, to them, there is only one Universe while the rest of beings face layers of multiverses, because they are at the infinite dimensions while we are at finite dimensions.

The Immeasurable

After learning the proofs of spiritual guides from various credible sources and understanding why some people could see them and communicate with them, I had a dream. In the dream, I was awakened from sleep. Then I was shocked to find a huge snake on my chest, moving slowly. I was afraid to move a bit and watched it slowly move to the bottom of my bed.

The second morning, I asked Google what a snake in the dream meant. The first answer gave me eight positive meanings and seven negative

---

[76] https://en.wikipedia.org/wiki/Pure_Land_Buddhism

meanings[77]. Since my life at this point was all positive except for the loss of my deeply beloved father, I chose to focus on the positive meanings. Here they are:

- Tapping into inner wisdom
- Symbol of empowerment
- Transitioning and transformation
- Sensual awakening
- Being mindful of the need for self-preservation
- Seeking a balance between rest and work
- Unveiling hidden knowledge
- Connection to the divine feminine

I resonated deeply with the interpretations, and the final one particularly struck a chord. My strong connection with my father fuels a profound desire to guide him on his spiritual journey. Given his staunch atheist belief during his lifetime, my conviction is that he may benefit from my assistance as he embarks on this new phase of existence. I am determined to lead him to the place of peace and spiritual fulfilment that he truly deserves. This act of love and devotion is my way of honoring his contribution

---

[77] https://www.worldofdreams.com/dream-dictionary/snakes-in-bed/

to my life and continuing our bond beyond this earthly realm.

I deeply regret the ignorance and stubbornness that had marked my spiritual journey. Driven by a profound longing to uncover the ultimate truth and reunite with Father, I embarked on a quest to select a religious path that would offer solace and guidance. My understanding was that, at their core, all major religions sought to illuminate the path to the ultimate truth from within, and my task was to find the one that resonated the most with my soul.

My exploration led me to consider Taoism[78], Buddhism and Christianity, the three traditions with which I had some familiarity. Initially, I leaned

---

[78] Taoism is a religion and a philosophy from ancient China that has influenced folk and national belief. Taoism has been connected to the philosopher Lao Tzu, who around 500 B.C.E. wrote the main book of Taoism, the *Tao Te Ching*. Taoism holds that humans and animals should live in balance with the Tao, or the universe. Taoists believe in spiritual immortality, where the spirit of the body joins the universe after death.

https://education.nationalgeographic.org/resource/taoism/#

toward Christianity, drawn to what appeared to be fewer restrictions and a more straightforward path. The prospect of navigating Buddhism's extensive list of restrictions and the vast trove of 6,000+ books of sutras felt daunting, as though it would require more lifetimes than I could conceive. Additionally, Taoism's requirement for new practitioners to spend at least two months in a dark room for repentance and the hundreds of restrictions struck me as a challenging commitment.

However, in February 2023, my course shifted once more, and I returned to Buddhism for three significant reasons. Foremost was my turbulent mind, which was besieged by guilt and tormenting memories of my failure to be present for Father during his greatest need. I needed to calm down and focus, but prayers couldn't help. I couldn't finish reading one page of the Bible without distraction.

Secondly, my experience with *The Bible* didn't help me connect with Father and lift him to heaven where he should belong. Still, the sutra of *The Original Vows of Ksitigarbha Bodhisattva*[79] offered

---

[79] http://www.drbachinese.org/online_reading_simplified/sutra_explanation/EarthStore/EarthStoreSutra.htm

incredibly effective solutions. Intrigued and hopeful, I embarked on a week-long journey with the dharma, and the results were nothing short of extraordinary.

Haunted by distressing nightmares of my Father in a state of suffering, I sought refuge in the practices I had discovered. I lighted fragrant incense and created a sacred space in front of the Buddha statue, inviting Father to join me. Then I read him the above sutra. I learned that after reading the sutra every day for seven days, I would witness my father in a dream, revealing his situation. Surprisingly, after I did this for only two days, Father came to my dream. He appeared in good shape this time. The dream unfolded in a magnificent, pristine environment reminiscent of the sacred landscapes described in the *Amitabha Sutra*.[80] After that, I always dreamed of Father in good shape.

Thirdly, my spiritual path directly led me to the top of all the Buddha's teachings, *The Lotus Sutra*.[81] It not only exposed that all sentient beings are

---

[80] https://purelanders.com/2013/01/02/amitabha-sutra/

[81] https://en.wikipedia.org/wiki/Lotus_Sutra

future Buddhas but also revealed another shocking truth that spared me from hesitation about choosing which path to take. In the chapter of *The Universal Gateway*, Avalokitesvara suggested that Buddhist disciples not to criticize the teachings of other religions because they could be delivered by the Buddhas in different forms, tailored to the needs and spiritual maturity of each society or each scient being at various stages.

It was a revelation[82] that echoed the wisdom of the venerable master Chin Kung, who once mentioned that Jesus Christ, God, and Allah could be the manifestations of Amitabha[83], a central figure in Pure Land Buddhism. I then realized that Jesus Christ and Amitabha both encouraged people to call upon their names when need help or want to go to the heavens when leaving the earth.

---

[82] https://youtu.be/8QMH30eO27I?si=uwc0pyP-sqapW8m4u

[83] https://www.metmuseum.org/art/collection/search/72419#:~:text=Amitayus%2C%20the%20Buddha%20of%20Eternal,of%20jewels%20and%20auspicious%20symbols.

As I delved deeper into my spiritual journey, my commitment to the unsurpassable, extremely profound, subtle, and wonderful Buddha Dharma grew stronger. I formally announced to my family about my dedication to becoming a devoted Buddhist. I vowed to spend the rest of my life or lives to understand the true meanings of the Buddha and help others to understand. I especially want to do this in English since most of the sutras are in Chinese or Tibetan language, and the translations into English made so many meanings lost. All my family members understood my need and respected my decision.

I joined a Buddhist Studies group sponsored by Bliss & Wisdom of America[84] via Zoom every Sunday and watched lectures on several of the most important Buddhist sutras by reputable monks from YouTube every day. I felt like a kid wandering in an immense amusement park, excited every day. I had never been like this before. Even when I made my first can of gold as a young woman, I was not as excited as today because the Buddha's immeasurable wisdom keeps expanding my horizon and showing

---

[84] https://www.us.blisswisdom.org/zh-hans/norcal/

me the ultimate reality of my True Self – the source of the Universe.

In *The Shurangama Sutra*[85], the merciful Buddha unveiled that everything in the Universe is a projection from the Mind. Not the mind in your head but the Mind of the Universe. The Mind has no form but omnipresent, omnipotent, and omniscient. However, due to the indulgence of our six senses, we mundane people made the ultimate truth and our reality upside down. We treat the ever-changing phenomenon as real existence; we treat the never-change ultimate truth, the formless but omnipotent conscious Mind, as nonexistent.

The merciful Buddha offered us the path to witness the ultimate truth by ourselves. He taught us how to climb up the stages of precepts, concentration, and enlightenment through observation, contemplation, and meditation in detail so that we could witness what he experiences.

---

[85] https://en.wikipedia.org/wiki/Śūraṅgama_Sūtra

The Avatamsaka Sutra[86] revealed a stunning revelation - that all Buddhas, whether of the past, present, and future, share one dharma body. *The Lotus Sutra*[87] revealed that all sentient beings are future Buddhas, and every sentient being is self-contained from within, no need to search for anything outside. In addition to the secret of no individual self and no death exposed in *The Heart Sutra*, with a bit of math skill, aha! Pointed out by the venerable master Chin Kung, "Throughout the cosmos, there is no one else but Yourself."

All existences in the cosmos share this one Mind/Universal Consciousness[88], just like how all terminators share one operating system on a mainframe computer. In this analogy, the passwords

---

[86] http://www.buddhism.org/Sutras/2/Avatamsaka_Sutra.htm

[87] https://www.sgi-usa.org/the-humanism-of-the-lotus-sutra/the-lotus-sutra/

[88] https://en.wikipedia.org/wiki/Universal_mind#:~:text=Universal%20mind%20or%20universal%20consciousness,and%20becoming%20in%20the%20universe.

required to access the infinite functions of The Mind correspond to one's vibrational frequency. The profound insight emerges that greater freedom is associated with a broader bandwidth of vibrational frequencies. For instance, for the spiritually enlightened, their vibration frequencies could be < 0.5 Hz and > 100 Hz simultaneously, whereas mundane people's bandwidth typically falls within the range of 1~30 Hz.

Reviewing the *Heart Sutra* again ten years later, I finally clicked on the concept of Śūnyatā[89], the coexistence of emptiness and existence. All the physical existences are just projections from the Mind of the Universe. None of them can independently exist.

I finally understood why we mundane people struggle to grasp the Buddha's insight into Śūnyatā and the absence of an individual self. These challenges can be attributed to several factors:

---

[89] The voidness that constitutes the ultimate reality; sunyata is seen not as a negation of existence but rather as the undifferentiation out of which all apparent entities, distinctions, and dualities arise.

https://www.britannica.com/topic/sunyata

1) Delusions: Often, we become fixated on the minutiae of our daily lives and fail to see the grand tapestry of the cosmos as a unified entity. Our preoccupation with the small details can obstruct our view of the bigger picture and the interconnectedness of all things.

2) Judging mindset: Our overactive left brain, driven by ego, tends to generate an endless stream of judgmental thoughts. These ego-driven thoughts are supposed to protect us, but they over consume our energy and time, left little room for us to listen to the wisdom of Nature – our True Self.

3) Attachment: Our strong attachments to false beliefs create a web of suffering. These attachments blind us to the transient nature of material possessions, relationships, and desires. In clinging to what is fleeting, we often overlook the enduring wisdom and serenity that the Buddha's teachings offer.

Recognizing these barriers is just the first step towards transcending them. Fortunately, the *Diamond Sutra* taught us how to let go of delusions, quiet the judging mind and release attachments. Thus, we can eventually end all suffering and obtain enlightenment and bliss.

After exploring a few of the Buddhist sutras, I was amazed at how extensive and profound the Buddha's teachings were. They go way beyond science, yet the dharmas are seriously scientific in terms of reasoning and evidence. They go way beyond science because the realm of the Buddhas can't be understood by reasoning. That doesn't mean we must blindly trust his words.

In fact, the Buddha Shakamuni requested his followers not to trust every word he said, because there were no words could accurately describe what he wanted to convey. One's understanding of his words could be totally different from what he meant to say. That's why he requested his followers to experience and witness the ultimate truth personally through the paths he offered.

Many people see the Buddha's teachings as a philosophy. I think it's very different from philosophy. Philosophy teaches people how to think. The Buddha's teachings not only cover how to think but also how to not think. The latter could be more important than the former because when you keep thinking, you can't observe profoundly and comprehensively. When you are thinking, you are judging and living on your limited ego. When you are observing, you are living on the non-judging Mind of the infinite Universe.

After studying *The Shurangama Sutra,* I quit all meat and a few other things because the wisdom within the sutra revealed to me the importance of adhering to the restrictions. Without the restrictions of our body, mouth, and mind, we can't have the great compassion and composure to achieve samadhi[90], a state of deep meditative consciousness, which is a condition to allow the wisdom of the universe to shine from our shared True Self. I want to be enlightened and help others who want to achieve enlightenment for the rest of my life/lives.

***

After observing such immense benefits from practicing Qi Gong and Buddhism, it's worth noting that they can indeed have adverse effects when approached with the wrong mindset or intentions. The

---

[90] https://en.wikipedia.org/wiki/Samadhi

pursuit of magic powers and personal gain while neglecting the core principles of kindness, compassion, and ethical conduct can lead individuals down a problematic path. When the ego takes precedence, it can lead to a distortion of the practice's true essence, causing harm to both the practitioner and others.

Practicing mindfulness, compassion, and ethical conduct alongside these disciplines can help ensure that individuals derive the intended benefits without encountering detrimental consequences. Balancing the pursuit of spiritual growth with a commitment to kindness and compassion is fundamental to a wholesome and rewarding practice.

Many documented experiences and studies cite instances of low-frequency spirits entering the human body. On many occasions, they were spirits from dead animals. Professor Lee's study report on Finger Reading mentioned such instances, and the venerable master Chin Kung also mentioned evil spirits attached to monks in his lecture on *The Avatamsaka Sutra*[91].

---

[91] https://youtu.be/97sMrj5w-rU?si=u5QwS6lmfAlkjwRK

In the article titled, *Example of Devil Enter Body After Practicing Qi Gong with Unpure Heart*[92], Mr. Li talked about his experience of letting four bad spirits enter his body and manipulate his body and mind while practicing Qi Gong. He was a well-read man and knew that in *The Shurangama Sutra*, the Buddha mentioned 50 different kinds of devils and warned his followers to avoid them. When Mr. Li felt his lifestyle was unhealthy, with unusual desire and no peace and satisfaction, he asked the Lord Jesus Christ to kick out the devils from his body. So, he was saved and became a Christian since then.

In an interview, Qi Gong master Cai[93] recounted a chilling and distressing account from his tenure as a high school teacher in Hong Kong. The narrative unfolded as a harrowing ordeal involving over 100 young boys who had fallen under the influence of malevolent spirits while engaging in Qi Gong practices. Through collaboration with a Christian

---

[92] https://www.dharmazen.org/X2GB/D33SProb/P4-238.htm

[93] https://youtu.be/N5u0cWKD-qk?si=2-2YA-LUkBNgwhPf

church, Master Cai and his colleagues eventually rescued the afflicted boys, but the events were alarming.

Mr. Cai, an adept Qi Gong master, insightfully highlights, "The highest frequency of the Universe is benevolence and spirits resonating with such energy are inherently compassionate and selfless." According to his perspective, these benevolent spirits respect an individual's free will but stand ready to help when earnestly requested. Conversely, those low-frequency malevolent spirits, who are prone to invading and taking advantage of individuals, are vulnerable to expulsion by the potent and benevolent spirits.

On Professor Lee's website[94], he categorizes individuals with Exceptional Ability into three distinct types. The first group comprises those who have successfully opened their Third Eye, indicating an elevated state of spiritual awareness. The second category involves individuals capable of experiencing Out of Body Experience, a phenomenon where one's consciousness temporarily separates from the physical body. The third kind encompasses individuals

---

[94] https://sclee.website/三種型式的特異功能人士/

with external spirits attached to their bodies, with the intriguing possibility that these spirits might originate from deceased animals.

The captivating tale of Finger Reading studies conducted in Yun Nan, China, in 2018, as narrated by Professor Lee, presents a fascinating illustration. The scholarly forum, where young children demonstrated their Finger Reading abilities, unfolds as both intriguing and thought-provoking.

Within the confines of the forum, Professor Lee initiated an interaction with a child, presenting a note that bore the question, "Where are you from? How should I address you?" The child conveyed that she heard a voice saying, "You may call me Xiao Zhang." Professor Lee then believed it was a spirit from someone who died young and attached to this kid. Professor Lee insisted it was not a good thing for this kid and that she should work on having her own Third Eye opened.

So, when exploring our innate treasures, we should always watch for our thoughts and always make sure that our thoughts are positive, kind, and compassionate. Otherwise, our low-frequency thoughts will attract those low-frequency energies into our lives and exhaust us. That is why we all need high-frequency spiritual guides. Those pure spirits, such as, the Buddha Shakamuni, Lao Tzu, Jesus Christ, Mother Teresa…are all for our help. All we need to do is sincerely call on their names and ask for help. They would unconditionally help us because they are essentially our True Self.

THREE STEPS TO MANIFEST

OUR DREAM

Everything is made from the Mind.

~The Buddha Shakamuni

Dear reader,

I finally understood that all my sufferings in the last decade were the projections from my ego, which has a delusional sense of "I" that trapped my mind in negative thoughts. My chaotic worries brought my mental pictures into reality and attracted more chaos from the others to make things worse.

The wisdom of the grand master Hui-Neng[95] inspired me to realize that we should worry about nothing because the Buddha nature that we all share is perfect and self-sufficient.

We can manifest anything. The Universe can rearrange the structure of spacetime to form our dreams, because our True Self is the Source/Mind of the Universe. The password is **Frequency.** Higher frequency means a higher degree of wisdom and freedom, as Dr. Margaret Paul pointed out[96].

When we find ourselves in a life we don't desire, it's because we live through our delusional egos, attuned to vibrations that do not serve us. It's time to tune into a higher-frequency channel that enriches us. By consistently elevating our frequency, we can transcend from turmoil to tranquility, aspiring toward the frequency of enlightenment.

Dear reader, I am so grateful that my pains guided me like light and brought me out from the

---

[95] https://terebess.hu/zen/HuinengCleary.pdf

[96] https://aspiremag.net/a-high-frequency-is-essential-for-at-will-divine-connection/

darkness to my dream life, a life full of love, compassion, and meaning. So, I summarized the three steps I took to manifest my dreams. I hope this can help you find your own unique path to Self-Realization.

Step 1: Raise Our Frequency

The brilliant Rhonda Byrne pointed out an important feature of human beings. That is, each of us has the function of a TV tower that can broadcast and receive signals. The difference is that a TV tower communicates with radio waves; we communicate with light waves (images), sound waves (sound), and consciousness. We need to practice for a long time to obtain the last skill efficiently, but almost every one of us has the first two skills.

However, one of the biggest challenges of Rhonda Byrne's suggested first step - Ask - is that when we are seriously troubled, we do not know what to ask because we are limited to our beliefs and our environment. For example, when I told my brother Li that his thoughts could make his dream come true, he responded, "Well, I think of money all the time; why don't money show up?"

Me, "What you had in mind was not money but easy money without putting in your effort. That was why you attracted people with the same thoughts into your life. So, they could have the chance to steal your money." Unfortunately, Brother Li lost his whole life savings to dishonest businesspeople at the beginning of the COVID-19 pandemic. He was one of the reasons I wrote this self-help book.

Although the Universe can deliver anything we ask, to ask for the right thing, we need wisdom. As the Buddha pointed out, wisdom comes from a clear and still mind, a clear and still mind comes from discipline. So, the first thing we need to do is discipline ourselves from the sources that caused us all the chaos. Thus, we stop synchronizing with them and switch to a new direction toward wisdom.

If we can't afford to leave the chaotic environment for the time being, we can stop responding to it and meditate. *Doing nothing is better than doing the wrong thing.* If we can't meditate with our habitual monkey mind, we can chant a mantra so we can reduce all the chaotic thoughts to one thought of the mantra.

There are many powerful mantras accessible online, and I plan to write another book detailing my remarkable experiences with certain Buddhist mantras. Among them, the mantra that has a profound impact on me is Avalokitesvara's *Six-Character Great Bright Mantra*: *"Om Mani Padme Hum,"* which translates to "pure like a lotus flower, in the power of Buddha." Despite not initially comprehending why and how it functions, this mantra provided me with immense strength during the toughest period of my life. Its extraordinary potency played a significant role in fostering my trust and appreciation for Buddhism. I would also suggest reading *The Mahayana Sublime Treasure King Sutra*[97] about this incredible mantra, it almost fixes everything.

When we stop engaging in our negative environment and calmly observe our surroundings, we naturally elevate our frequency by no longer entangling ourselves with low vibrations. From this point, we can continue to raise our frequency steadily, inching closer toward full-scale Self-Realization.

---

[97] http://read.goodweb.net.cn/news/news_view.asp?newsid=14903

After we have calmed our minds, we tell ourselves, "From now on, I will only focus on the positive things, be aware of the negative things that are happening, but never respond to them except in emergencies. I am so grateful that I can breathe. As I observe my breathing, my life is regenerating…"

Now, we can *envision a mission-oriented life*. That means, a life to give our seeds of love and compassion, our service, and our creative products to our family, friends, community…the world, and the universe. Envision a service or product that we can passionately and tirelessly work on improving and that our loved ones would appreciate. Envision the details of our dream service or product. Envision how and where we will get each part of our dream service or product. If we can't envision a clear image in our mind, search from the internet. We are so fortunate to live in this amazing age of technology advancement.

For example, I wanted to make a Mapo Tofu for my family. I looked at a few videos on YouTube, remembered the recipe, and adjusted it to fit my new vegetarian needs. Then I searched for where I could find all the ingredients. Then, I followed the steps to make my little dream come true.

Big dreams are comprised of smaller ones. By concentrating on what we already possess, we can rearrange our resources to manifest larger and larger dreams. It's crucial to disregard what we lack because when we concentrate on nurturing what we have, we align ourselves with individuals vibrating at higher frequencies who would assist us in realizing our aspirations. Focusing on what we lack only squanders our precious time, which could otherwise be devoted to elevating our frequency and pursuing meaningful dreams or just enjoy peace.

Step 2: Broadcast

Now we have a beautiful and sweet dream, a big one. It's time to invite helpers to make our dreams come true because no big dream can be realized by anyone single-handedly. How do we do that?

We do that by improving our communication skills. First, we stop complaining and be mindful of what we say and do, stay positive and keep our behaviors consistent with our dreams. If my dream is to be a pianist, but I don't practice every day, that is not consistent. If my dream was to be Ken's wife, but I didn't want to do anything for him or with him, that would not be consistent. Such dreams are not from my heart but from my ego. Make dreams that are from our heart so we can manifest them effortlessly.

Then, we mention the keywords of our dream to our family, friends, colleagues, social media, conventional media, search engines…, and even in our prayers, so the Universe knows what we want. Those who resonate with us will synchronize with us; the unrelated will gradually disappear. Later, we will realize that everyone around us wants to nurture us.

To surpass even our loftiest aspirations, we must embrace the principle of sowing what we desire, for we reap what we sow, magnified. Craving assistance? Extending our hand first, without strings attached, for assistance with expectations is not genuine aid; it's a transaction. Yearning for love? Shower others with pure love unconditionally. The wider the spectrum of beings we envelop with our affection, the higher our frequency ascends, thus more blossoming from our perfect and self-sufficient True Self.

Seeking wisdom? Share the insights of the wise generously, aiding the enlightenment of others and enrichment of the world. When our spirit is mature, the wise mentor will manifest in our lives, illuminating our path with profound teachings. Through selfless giving, we become conduits of abundance, kindness, and enlightenment, enriching not just our lives but the entire tapestry of existence.

Desiring financial abundance? Then, generously nurture individuals or enterprises with what we can afford. In Chinese, there is a word - 舍得 - that defies direct translation into English. Its first character signifies "give up," while the second denotes "gain." Together, it embodies the concept of "giving up to gain." This word extends beyond mere charity; it encompasses the virtue of generosity, supporting individuals and businesses alike. In the Taoist teachings, there is an idiom: 心死神活 (mind die, spirit come alive). That means, we must empty our mind to let our omniscient and omnipotent spirit[98] to function. Our mind is intelligent and know the differences, but the wise one is our spirit which is compassionate and owns the Universe.

---

[98] According to the Taoist teachings, each person has three kinds of spirits, totally 12 of them. I will talk about this in the next book.

If we all adopted a frugal lifestyle and refrained from spending, businesses would wither away. Of course, I am not advocating extravagance. Instead, I propose embracing propriety in our actions—striking a balance between prudence and generosity, ensuring that our resources are wisely invested in endeavors that uplift individuals and communities alike.

Step 3. Receive

Twenty years ago, when I was in a TOEFL preparation class in my hometown of Chongqing, a beautiful 17-year-old girl wrote an English paper starting with a line like this: "Success is a shy girl; *she only smiles to those who are prepared.*" That line stayed in my mind forever.

Our first two steps are so important and powerful that they must be implemented to manifest our dreams. The universe takes orders by the forms of image and sound, and we did both with clarity and coherence, gracefully. Congratulations! We made our orders; now it's time to receive them.

When we tune in to watch a BBC program, we align ourselves with its frequency channel.

THE JOURNEY TO AWAKENING

Similarly, when it comes to receiving our dreams, we must maintain a vibration frequency that matches the dreams we deserve. Good luck isn't happenstance – it's a reflection of our alignment with the frequencies of our aspirations.

That means being grateful for what we already have and appreciating every moment of life, every breath, every step forward, every drop of rain, every sunrise, every star, every smile, every hug, every grain of rice, every bird's singing, every tree that provides shade and inspiration...

Be mindful, patiently and confidently observe the seeds of our dreams as they grow, responding appropriately and without haste for quick outcomes. Just as chemically assisted tomatoes lack the flavor and nutrients of naturally grown ones, forcing results often yields inferior outcomes. Changing ourselves is challenging; changing others is nearly impossible. Trusting in ourselves is far more reliable than placing trust in others.

When the time is ripe, harvest our dreams with gratitude, expressing our love for the deliveries with words and big smiles. By doing so, the Universe recognizes our appreciation and will deliver more blessings. These blessings then serve our greater dreams, making the world a better place. Without gratitude, the Universe may cease deliveries, as it doesn't know what makes us happy. The Universe wants us to be happy. Thus, let us remain ever grateful!

AFTERWORD

"We should discover our True Self so that we can be leaders of light, hope, joy, and love for others."
- Dr. John D. Young[99]

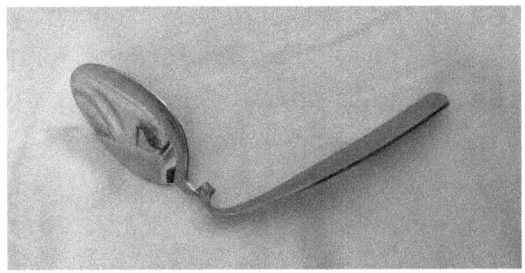

After finishing the first draft of this book, to prove the concept that *Everything has consciousness* - 万物皆有灵 - to my atheist husband Ken, I did an experiment with my mind.

I bent a spoon in my hands with the help of my mind. When I showed the spoon to Ken, he said, "It's no big deal," and bent another spoon with his

---

[99] https://www.taiwan-panorama.com/Articles/Details?Guid=e7ebe7ae-ac11-44d9-b70c-8b11d6a4231d&langId=3&CatId=11

hands. Then, I asked him to twist the spoon. He tried but no success.

So, I took the spoon to try whether I could twist it. Of course, I twisted the spoon twice, expectingly, with the help of my mind. Then I showed it to Ken; he still could not believe it.

Then, I posted the picture and the story of the spoon in my WeChat friend circle. Our Study Queen from Chongqing Bashu High School, Susan, who is now an IT expert in the US, commented, "Can you do this in front of me?" Then she added, "If this is true, it will up end a lot of people's beliefs."

Understood her disbelief, I said, "You can do this by yourself; everybody can. You just need a focused mind and communicate with the spoon sincerely. Try more times if you didn't succeed at the first try." Then, I told her about the steps in more detail.

"You pick a spoon that you can't bend to do the experiment. Otherwise, you wouldn't know whether your mind helped the process.

"Then you touch the place you want it to bend and talk to the spoon, 'Please do me a favor; let me bend you.' Then envision the spot you touched to become soft, soft, soft...like a noodle, then you bend it with both of your hands."

Two days later, she sent me a picture.

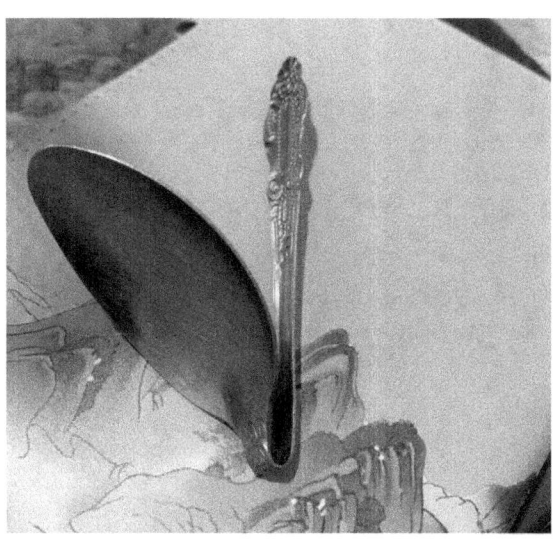

Then, another picture.

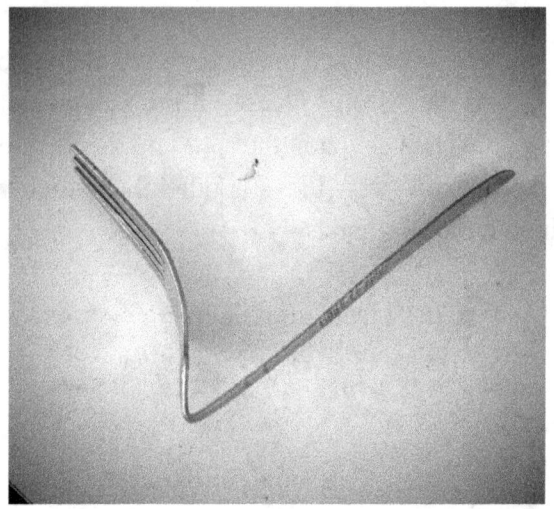

So, I said, "Be careful; we are already out of spoons for dinner."

Susan, "Now we both become spoon destroyers."

Me, "hope we don't cause a spoon shortage in the US."

One month later, she was on a trip to the Caucasus and sent me a picture on Wechat:

THE JOURNEY TO AWAKENING

So, I asked her, "do you bend a spoon every day?"

Susan, "I also tried to bend someone else's spoon, but didn't succeed. That one was hard."

Later, she sent another picture and said, "that one started to bend too."

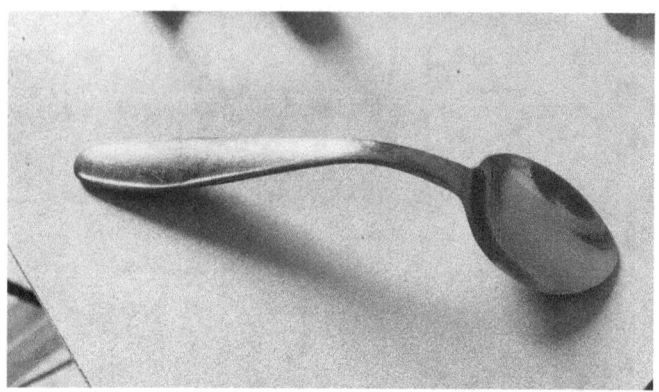

Dear reader,

    The potential of our spirit/shared True Self is infinite. We just need to let go of our ego, keep an open and compassionate heart, and then unlearn the belief that limited us. It's not easy at the beginning, but we are fortunate to have such profound and comprehensive Buddha dharmas to enlighten our paths. So, the road to Self-Realization would be much easier than travelling in the dark.

    No big dream can be achieved alone. This book would have been impossible without the unconditional love and support of my parents, especially my father, Deng Ji Xiang, and my beloved husband, Ken Cera. Although Father can't talk to me anymore, his loving energy has always been synchronized with mine.

THE JOURNEY TO AWAKENING

This book would not have been possible without the Web of brilliant Stars who are life scientists and Buddhist/Taoist masters. They inspired me to revisit those ancient scripts of the Sages who helped me to realize that the ultimate truth of the Universe and life are not secret. The dharmas were systematically taught by ancient Sages and numerous dedicated wisdom seekers witnessed and documented precisely. These ancient teachings are beyond science and philosophy, because the latter two only look outward for truth while the former observe both outward and inward. These ancient teachings aren't just theories, they were firsthand experiences and can be experienced by any sincere truth seekers.

These brilliant modern stars enlightened me and my talented editor, Anna Watson, who I had so much fun working with in the past year.

I am eternally grateful for all their contributions to my growth. I have no way to repay their generosity but following their path to enlightenment and be the light for the world. I used to be an award-winning peer mentor when I was in college. I will use my talent to help the English speakers to understand the profound Buddha dharmas.

Dear reader, I hope you have found inspiration from this book. If you choose to explore Buddhism more, you are welcome to join our community on Facebook@jinlancera, where like-minded people share their questions and insights on the way to our self-realization. We may even meditate together to strengthen our spiritual power through synchronicities. You may also follow me on X@jinlancera and YouTube@jinlancera; I will periodically share my experience of practicing Buddha dharmas on these platforms. Thank you so much for reading my book. May you have a magnificent life!

THE JOURNEY TO AWAKENING

Avalokistesvara Bodhisattva's Six-Character Great Bright Mantra in Tibetan language

Avalokitesvara Bodhisattva

www.ingramcontent.com/pod-product-compliance
Lightning Source LLC
Chambersburg PA
CBHW070736020526
44118CB00035B/1371